HOLY LEISURE

T0289525

HOLY LEISURE

Recreation and Religion in God's Square Mile

Troy Messenger

Temple University Press
Philadelphia

Temple University Press, Philadelphia 19122
www.temple.edu/tempress
Copyright 1999 by the Regents of the University of Minnesota

All rights reserved.

First published in hardcover by the University of Minnesota Press

Paperback edition published 2000 by Temple University Press

Printed in the United States of America

⊗ The paper used in this publication meets the minimum requirements of American National Standard for Information Sciences—Permanence of Paper for Printed Library Materials, ANSI/NISO Z39.48-1992.
Manufactured in the United States of America.

Library of Congress Cataloging-in-Publication Data

Messenger, Troy.
    Holy leisure : recreation and religion in God's square mile / Troy
Messenger.
        p.   cm.
    Originally published: Minneapolis : University of Minnesota Press, c1999.
    Includes bibliographical references (p.) and index.
    ISBN 1-56639-841-X (pbk. : alk. paper)
    1. Ocean Grove New Jersey Camp Meeting Association—History.
    2. Recreation—Religious aspects—Methodist Church—History of doctrines.
    3. Recreation—New Jersey—Ocean Grove—History.   4. Ocean Grove
(N.J.)—Church history.   I. Title.

BX8476.02M47   2000
287'.674946—dc21   00-034348

ISBN 13: 978-1-56639-841-1 (pbk. : alk. paper)

042809P

For Wilma and Ari

CONTENTS

PROLOGUE: A DAY IN GOD'S SQUARE MILE

I awake once again at half past five to my son's insistent pleas. But instead of ducking under the pillow as I might in our New York City apartment, I quickly jump up to satisfy his need for attention. He is just shy of his first birthday, and reasoning is futile. Even though we're not in one of the campground tents, his early morning entreaties easily penetrate the Methodist walls of nineteenth-century seaside architecture. Here in the Sampler Inn, a Victorian-era boarding hotel on the New Jersey shore, sleeping patterns are of communal concern. Walls in the compact rooms are barely more than transparent. Bedroom doors stand open to the nocturnal ocean breezes drifting down the hall. The gently fluttering doorway curtains offer some modesty, but little in the way of security or privacy.

Opting to let my wife grab a few more minutes of sleep, Ari and I make for the street. Main Avenue is still asleep. Almost. Though the smells of bacon, eggs, and coffee are already wafting from the Sampler kitchen, the cafeteria doesn't open until seven. The Main Avenue bakery does, however, offer simple fare for those like myself who can't wait for the few other restaurants to open.

Across the street, a small cluster of people are shuffling through the stacks of morning newspapers. Inside, there is even a short line past the popular magazines and romance novels. I think to myself that William Osborn and Rev. Ellwood Stokes would probably not have considered much of this edifying reading. Surely they would have gasped at the rows of cigarettes and the lottery-ticket dispenser.

Ari and I retreat to the boardwalk for our breakfast. It has been a hot summer, and already it is beginning to warm up. Occasional joggers and dog walkers exchange friendly greetings with me. Soon, dedicated beach goers arrive with wagons full of towels, toys, umbrellas, books, and assorted other beach paraphernalia. By midday, the sun worshippers will be thick on the clean white sands.

By nine o'clock, Ari is back with his mom, and I am at the Tabernacle Bible Hour. The doors are attended by members of the Auditorium Ushers, and I am given another "Good morning, how are you." Outside camp-meeting week, these morning Bible Hours attract a few dozen faithful. At nearly forty, I'm one of the few "young" congregants. The service follows a familiar format. We sing light music—a couple of old gospel favorites and some newer choruses to which people can raise their hands. A few people do. But respectfully so. Unlike their frontier antecedents, nobody shouts anything, jerks, or asks me to. After a few announcements that echo the multicolored montage of photocopied flyers posted outside, ushers quickly collect the morning dollars.

While a local pastor teaches the Bible passage—preaches, actually—I take in the century-old Tabernacle architecture. I imagine the walls removed and my pew a rough-hewn plank. I picture myself before a nineteenth-century preacher's stand in the woods. Even with the crackly sound system, there is something in this form that recalls a piety of another time and place.

Afterward, my laptop and I make our daily walk to the Asbury Park library to read microfilm reels of the *Ocean Grove Times*. Walking north on the boardwalk, I cross the mouth of Wesley Lake, which separates Ocean Grove from Asbury. The landscape changes immediately. In Asbury, the decaying shells of fairground-baroque structures stand at the water's edge. The marvelously intricate ironwork of the carousel building houses the leftovers of a weekend flea market. The airplane-hangar-size skating rink still bears the imprint of advertisements from a more prosperous era. Another building bears a sign reading "Asbury Casino." Lower on the wall the words "City of Asbury Park Places of worship" are still visible, even though someone has painted over them. Nearby a half-completed high-rise apartment building stands among weeds and concrete slabs. Visible through the dusty window of a boardwalk office is a model of the abandoned project, mocking the failed dreams of overzealous developers.

On my return, I stop in for an ice cream at Days, the same ice-cream parlor popular with the 1870s crowds I have just read about; restoration of

Figure 1. On this vacant building adjacent to the Asbury Park carousel are signs for both the Asbury Casino and the City of Asbury Park Places of worship. Photograph by Troy Messenger.

the landmark restaurant is almost complete. In fact, there seems to be construction and renovation under way on every block. Around the corner and down the street, the Ocean Plaza Hotel is also alive with the sounds of power saws and hammers. The omnipresence of Gannon Contractors' trucks in Ocean Grove, the volunteers painting the boardwalk railings, and the carefully tended plants before every tent contrast starkly with the decaying boardwalk of Asbury.

Back down at the beach, the scene is a microcosm of contemporary Ocean Grove. Although several hundred people line the waterfront, an eerie silence pervades the air. An ice-cream truck coasts to a stop, serves a customer, and then noiselessly moves on down the street.

Finally, the afternoon gospel-music show gets cranked up at the beach pavilion. It turns out to be a man in his fifties singing pop Christian tunes to tape tracks on a portable Karaoke amp. A few people like myself stay anyway, since this is the only free shade on the beach. Between songs, we get a running testimony of God's power and some not-so-subtle exhortations to turn from our sins.

When I look to my left across the beach, a woman in a bright red bikini catches my eye. On the sand, next to her, a friend lies face down on her towel, her bikini top undone. I wonder how Victorian women in their dark, heavy, wool bathing dresses could have survived hundred-degree summer days. I also let myself imagine those Victorian women meeting the two women on the beach. Or perhaps the two guys over there who are obviously more than friends.

It is hard to reconcile these contrasting images, but they exist throughout Ocean Grove. Evangelical preaching next to hundreds of people enjoying the sun and surf. A resort on the Jersey shore where you can't buy a beer.

Once the concert is over, I head back to the Sampler. We have to hit the line at the cafeteria soon; at 4:45, it already stretches down the side of the building. We've been caught before looking in vain for a hot meal after 8 P.M. The McDonald's in Neptune is a long walk.

We move quickly through the line, picking a few familiar favorites. The Sampler Cafeteria is a good family eating place, by which I mean they don't seem to mind too much about a lot of noise and food on the floor. Besides, Ari loves their baked squash and their macaroni and cheese. My smothered pork chops are not exactly gourmet, but at something like five dollars a person, the price is right. The name of the inn comes from the many cross-stitched "samplers" displayed about the dining room bearing mottoes like "Home Sweet Home" and the Lord's Prayer.

After dinner, Ari chases pigeons on the wide grassy median of Ocean Pathway, while Wilma and I watch a group of people slowly putting more and more kites on several lines tethered to signs on the median. By half past seven, the town is winding down. Wilma and Ari head back for baths and bedtime rituals.

I'm back at the pavilion with a hundred others for the Ocean Grove Band's first Wednesday performance of the summer. The opening march transports me again out of twentieth-century New Jersey. Sousa by the sea. When the forty-piece ensemble moves on to an eclectic mix of Gershwin, show tunes, Bach, and Beethoven, my mind clears to find an odd collection of amateur musicians playing cello lines on euphonium and piano riffs on clarinet. By the time the band gets to its closing marches, a respectable rainstorm has blown in off the ocean. Those who came late and didn't get a seat quickly disperse. The rest of us pull up our coats and sit it out. The storm takes up its part between the piccolos and trumpets. The driving rain on the backs of the musicians quickens the tempos and rises in a crescendo through the last Trio. I'm on my feet. It's been a good concert, for both the band and the elements.

And it's been a good day. Pleasant company. Good beaches. Two sermons. Productive research. A great storm. All in a wonderfully manicured Victorian environment. What could be more perfect?

ACKNOWLEDGMENTS

I particularly want to thank my wife, Wilma, and son, Ari, for the support and patience they have shown me while I have worked on this manuscript.

Thanks also go to the faculty, staff, and students of the Performance Studies Department at New York University for their encouragement and feedback. Barbara Kirshenblatt-Gimblett has been instrumental in focusing my thinking and helping me translate these ideas into text. Richard Schechner offered a valuable perspective based both on his experience with ritual performance and on his family's presence in Ocean Grove and neighboring Bradley Beach for much of this century. Brooks McNamara helped me understand leisure in Ocean Grove in relation to other developments in popular entertainment and environmental performance. I am also extremely grateful to Nancy Ammerman, Randall Balmer, and Barbara Browning for their close reading and insightful comments. A special word of thanks goes to Matthew Abbate for his copyediting, critical advice, and unwavering friendship since the inception of this project.

Richard Gibbons commented to me that dozens of people have come to him in the past half-century working on everything from elementary-school research papers to books and films about Ocean Grove. Several of these have contributed significantly to the present study. Glenn Uminowicz's article on respectable recreation was an excellent introduction for me to the role of leisure in Ocean Grove and its connectedness to the holiness movement. Jennifer Boyd and John Sosenko allowed me to view their unreleased film on

Ocean Grove early in my research; this excellent footage documents the early 1980s, when the community was undergoing its transition in governance. More recently, Ted Bell has been very helpful in arranging interviews and commenting on this material.

A final word of thanks goes to the people of Ocean Grove who have made this research possible: to Tom Rechlin for his hospitality at the Sampler Inn in 1993 and 1994, the ushers and the marvelous choreography of their march, the Historical Society for access to their archives, the Ocean Grove Band, tent residents, beachcombers, and my neighbors on the other side of very thin walls who tolerated my son's sleeping schedule in the first year of his life.

PART I
THE CAMP MEETING AT OCEAN GROVE

1

SETTING THE STAGE

"Enter into his gates with thanksgiving and into his courts with praise," declares the main entrance to Ocean Grove, New Jersey. Although these gates no longer guard against the intrusion of undesirables or Sunday vehicular traffic, even at the turn of the twenty-first century, one cannot enter Ocean Grove without crossing boundaries, exiting one world, entering another, and stepping onto holy ground.

In July 1869, twenty people made the first pilgrimage to this overgrown, uninhabited patch of land. Before they left, they consecrated the sand dunes and shrub brush as sacred ground, a site for the faithful to come generation after generation to seek holiness. It may seem odd to an early-twenty-first-century reader to equate a place on the Jersey shore with the Holy Land; but for these twenty people, and for the hundreds of thousands who followed them, a stay in Ocean Grove was indeed a visit to the Holy. A summer lived in community with fellow pilgrims was time out of time—a sacred, festival time—when the routines of everyday life were put aside for the pursuit of perfection.

Ocean Grove and its people moved toward perfection by performing it. Within a carefully crafted architecture of holiness, a community of men and women created an intertwined system of models through which they made perfection both visible and a real possibility in present reality. Modeling perfection was a means of acting perfect while becoming perfect. The models presented officially sanctioned norms of holiness in ways that were

Figure 2. A communion service in the Great Auditorium. Reprinted from souvenir postcard, mid-twentieth century.

comprehensible. The models were not, however, static. They became ritual objects and actions—"means of grace," in Methodist terms—that helped produce the state being modeled. The performances of holiness created by the leaders of the community and facilitated by this unique performance space allowed large numbers of guests to model perfection together.

Ocean Grove was the longest-lived ecclesiarchy in American history. From its founding in 1869 until 1979, it operated under a charter that granted the Methodists of the Ocean Grove Camp Meeting Association municipal powers to create a utopian village that offered safe haven from the demands of the city. In its heyday, tens of thousands lived through the summer in a tent-and-cottage community carefully secluded and protected from the everyday world. Ocean Grove was a place where the rules of the everyday no longer applied. Yet unlike other nineteenth-century seaside resorts such as Atlantic City and Coney Island, noted for their air of carnival-like abandon, the rules at Ocean Grove were comparatively prohibitive. You could not drink. You could not smoke. You could not play cards. You could not drive your car on Sunday. You could, however, do several things that would have scandalized pious Methodists of an earlier era. You could, for example, enjoy the beach, take the summer off, sell tickets to popular amusements, and stage comic gender satire with cross-dressed men. But only if these things led you closer to the goal of perfection in holiness. The social architects of Ocean

Grove intended that every activity of the day and night would aid in the pursuit of holiness. Even recreation was an essential means of grace for the industrial-age urban worker. The model citizen in the model city did not have to spend every ounce of strength pursuing a secular occupation; instead, he or she had time to enjoy the fruits of God's creation and seek spiritual renewal. For a century and a quarter, residents of this community have performed this model of holiness by praying *and* playing together. Ocean Grove is Jerusalem-by-the-sea—a Holy City set apart from the quotidian—dedicated to perfection through holy leisure.

Ocean Grove was founded by members of the National Camp Meeting Association for the Promotion of Holiness. Today, two centuries after the explosive growth of camp meetings in America, thousands still make their pilgrimage to Ocean Grove every summer for a week-long camp-meeting revival by the sea. Camp meeting, the ubiquitous religious and social gathering ground of nineteenth-century frontier America, may sound like an anachronism as America begins the twenty-first century, when the frontier refers to other planets, quantum computing, and biotechnology. Yet throughout America, camp meetings remain an enduring phenomenon. Kenneth Brown has been able to document more than 120 active camp meetings founded in 1876 or earlier.[1] These contemporary camp meetings might appear to be historical dramas that replay and reassert nineteenth-century spirituality and culture in the light of American postmodernity. But for many participants, they remain an essential ritual of summer—a means of defining self and community.

Historians of religion have often marked the golden age of camp meetings as the beginning of the nineteenth century. Charles Johnson's classic work is typical of the popular thesis on their origin and decline. In his analysis, Presbyterian minister James McGready virtually invented camp meetings in Kentucky at the turn of the nineteenth century with his huge gatherings at Cane Ridge. "The origins of the camp meeting, which seemed to have appeared on the American frontier full blown in 1800 as the most striking manifestation of the Great Revival, have long been hid in obscurity. . . . One day the frontier was a godless place . . . and the next it was all aflame with religious zeal."[2] Johnson goes on to chart the tremendous success Methodists had in adopting the camp meeting as their own and using it to propagate their denomination throughout the trans-Allegheny West. But, he concludes, "The backwoods revival was apparently over by the 1840s. The once-great institution had reached the final stage of gradual but inevitable decline."[3] He attributes this decline to the changing demographics of America, with its improved transportation and refined social life, the overorganization of the institution in the thirties and forties by well-meaning Methodist leaders, the increasing emphasis on respectability, and the rise of alternative evangelistic tools like the protracted indoor meeting. Nowhere is this decline more evident for Johnson than in the publication of camp-meeting manuals in the 1840s and 1850s. Publishing only in the east, "their preacher-authors constituted a rear-guard action, a conservative phalanx battling to preserve the old. They insisted upon the continuance of the institution for its own sake."[4] In Johnson's view, permanent camp meetings like Ocean Grove were essentially resort communities that used the camp-meeting formula to great "commercial," if not religious, success.

Kenneth Brown challenges the notion that camp meetings flourished for only three or four decades on the frontier.[5] He argues that the prevalence of outdoor religious events in America from the mid-eighteenth century on means that the camp meeting could not have erupted *ex nihilo* in the fully developed form of the Kentucky revivals. The founders of Methodism, John Wesley and George Whitefield, themselves pioneered the use of outdoor spaces for preaching and sacramental services.[6] Other denominations held services outdoors when church buildings were either inadequate or non-existent. Further, Brown documents that, by 1794, a half-dozen years before Cane Ridge, these various outdoor services and meetings had evolved into genuine camp meetings at Grassy Bank and Denver, North Carolina.

Russell Richey argues in a similar vein that the Methodist practice of quarterly meetings provided a performance model that easily evolved into camp meetings. In these outdoor meetings, which preceeded what we know as camp meetings, Methodists from many parishes gathered members from throughout the region both to conduct the church's business and to stoke the fires of revival.[7] Richey states that "some of the camp meeting's power to create frontier community derived from its ritual reenactment of earlier Methodist community. It was a new way of reliving the old and an old way for living in the new."[8] After 1801, Methodists continued to gather by region, but the business portion of their gatherings was separated from the religious and was done at "conference." The religious element of these gatherings became camp meetings. The new mode of meeting "worked" for Methodists as for no other denomination precisely because it was not new but was rooted in familiar performance.

This new research on the origin of camp meetings highlights the important connection between Methodism and the genre of performance known paradigmatically in the frontier camp meeting. These scholars have shown that this performance idiom recurs consistently throughout the history of Methodism and is not confined to a singular expression of camp meeting prevalent on the frontier at the beginning of the nineteenth century. Rather, the camp meeting is related to other performances extending back to the days of Wesley and continuing beyond the frontier to include holiness resorts on the eastern seaboard, the educational assemblies at Chautauquas, and the myriad denominational campgrounds and meetings operating to the present day. Methodism did not co-opt the Presbyterian model. Although Presbyterians and Baptists did, in fact, continue to use camp meetings and revivals, the phenomenon, and its precursors and successors, was essential to the piety and polity of Methodism. As Methodism gained acceptability in the urban east, it did not abandon this important means for performing piety.

Johnson correctly notes that camp meetings underwent a profound metamorphosis at midcentury. But his assessment of later camp meetings as merely attempting to maintain the form without the substance fails to take seriously an important theological movement of the second half of the nineteenth century that rejuvenated the mature camp meetings of the northeast. The doctrine of "perfection" or "entire sanctification" is present in the writings of Wesley and his Methodist contemporaries, particularly John Fletcher. But with the calls from 1839 on for "special" publications, meetings, and preaching on this topic alone, the doctrine assumes a prominence that profoundly affected the practice of piety for Methodists throughout the remainder of the nineteenth century.

Wesley's writings contain no systematic theology and thus no complete— or, for that matter, completely consistent—treatment of the doctrine of perfectionism. Although his pragmatic responses to issues raised by his followers "contain" his theology, his writing often only treats the aspect of the doctrine relevant to the topic at hand. Thus, the holiness theology of Wesley has many names—sanctification, holiness, perfect love, freedom from sin, and Christian perfection. But the doctrine of perfectionism pervades his writings. Wesley and many of his followers claimed that perfectionism was the unique theological contribution of Methodism. Of perfectionism, he said, "This doctrine is the grand depositum which God has lodged with the people called Methodists; and for the sake of propagating this chiefly He appeared to have raised us up."[9] Wesley himself never claimed to have reached perfection, although he did not discount the testimony of others that they had been able to attain it.

Wesley's doctrine of sanctification stands in contrast both to the Catholic notion that purification begins in this life and continues in the next and to the Calvinist and Lutheran understanding of the Christian as forgiven but still sinning until death, when sanctification is immediately granted. Wesley began his pursuit of holiness in the Catholic tradition of an "improving" holiness. In fact, he often encouraged the reading of accounts by Catholic mystics of their search for perfection. But the most striking of Wesley's concepts was the possibility of "imparted" holiness—what his followers were to call a "second blessing." Not only could a sinner be immediately forgiven of sin but that person also could be instantaneously cleansed of the *possibility* of sinning. Sin in this sense meant a fracture in the continual love of God. Freedom from sin was not a freedom from mistakes; one could still make mistakes due to ignorance, be subject to temptations, and suffer infirmities of the body. Perfection did mean that a person might live in an unbroken conscious dependence upon God and attain, in this life, a state in which the soul was fully prepared for its eternal existence.

Wesley describes conversion and perfection as the two pivotal experiences in a person's religious life. In Wesleyan theology, particularly as it evolved in the late nineteenth century, these two events occur at specific and discernible moments. After the first—that is, conversion—Wesley calls his disciples to use every means of grace at their disposal to seek the second—perfection. The efforts to create various means to effectively facilitate conversion and perfection account for many of the distinctive practices among Methodists in the eighteenth and nineteenth centuries. John Wesley and some of his classmates at Oxford met regularly to read devotional books, pray, and hold each other accountable for their progress in perfection. This seemed excessive to their peers, who first used the name Methodist to denigrate them. But the group was so important to Wesley that he later admonished all his followers to meet weekly in similar groups, called classes or societies. Admittance to the group was open to all who desired "to flee the wrath to come"—that is, whose souls were ready for conversion. In the meetings, groups of a dozen or so would sing, give an account of their souls (literally a confession to the group), receive exhortation, pray over the specific needs of the group, and receive an offering.

Methodist class meetings and societies remained an active practice throughout the early-nineteenth-century period of frontier revivalism. In fact, a common practice at the early camp meetings was to live in "society tents" rather than family tents. The society model remained an influential paradigm for Methodism as it moved from the frontier to urban respectability. The accountability of society members to one another, their mutual exhortation, and their regular use of every available means of grace in moving members to conversion and perfection formed the basis for the performances of holy leisure at Ocean Grove. The piety of parlor-society meetings was instrumental in creating the need for permanent holiness camp meetings and in forming the patterns of devotion within these camp meetings.

During the Second Great Awakening, until at least 1830, the emphasis in both the society tent and on the mourners' bench was on the first of Wesley's two blessings—that is, the conversion experience. Dickson Bruce Jr. notes how the setting, hymnody, preaching, exhortation, and exercises of frontier camp meetings were carefully orchestrated toward a single goal—conversion. "The preachers did not want something—anything—to happen to the convert. Rather, they wanted a particular kind of interaction to occur between the individual and the divine. The form of the camp-meeting ensured this, for it was a collective expression of the pattern of conversion which the preachers had set down."[10] The form was, in fact, highly successful in converting thousands of people into the ranks of Methodism. If these early camp meetings were a collective performance of conversion, the camp meetings of the second half of the century facilitated a communitywide performance of perfection.

Wesley's second blessing—a growth in holiness toward entire sanctification—did not receive much attention in the first wave of camp meetings. Perfectionism in America was indeed on the rise in the early nineteenth century—but in social-reform movements like the Oneida community.[11] Accounts from the period indicate that within Methodism itself, the experience was "rarely met with" and in "danger of being regarded as a novelty."[12] This low point for perfectionism coincided with the beginning of the decline of revivalism in the west. In the minds of holiness advocates, the infrequency of the experience of holiness was directly responsible for the state of evangelism.[13] However, from about 1835, a group of ministers and laity began to preach the doctrine of perfection with the same evangelical fervor that previously had been applied to the conversion experience alone. Although these efforts were highly successful, they did have their critics. It was unusual for Methodists to form organizations around the "special" promotion of a single point of doctrine.[14] Critics feared that holiness would be promoted to the exclusion of other essential doctrines of the faith. Many Methodist authorities also felt threatened by the proliferation of these "special" activities outside the purview of the church. Largely lay initiated and controlled, holiness groups created parachurch organizations that challenged the role of the clergy as arbiters of Methodist theology and the church as the medium for contact with the holy. The publication of Timothy Merritt's *Guide to Christian Perfection* in 1839 is notable in that it called for semimonthly "*special* meetings of the church. . . . [T]he importance of the subject demands *special* attention and extra effort at this time."[15]

Probably the most instrumental *special* meeting for the promotion of holiness was a society meeting that began in 1835 at the home of the recently "perfected" Sarah Lankford. With her sister Phoebe Palmer, Lankford invited prayer groups she sponsored at the Allen Street and Mulberry Street Methodist Episcopal Churches to meet in her parlor at 54 Rivington Street, New York City. Lankford and Palmer's experiences of sanctification provided direction and model for the other members of the group. Although the group operated outside official sanction of any Methodist body, these Tuesday meetings drew heavily on the example of Wesleyan societies. Like other society meetings, Palmer's holiness meetings included prayer, testimony, exhortation, and singing, all with the goal of moving the participants toward greater holiness. The unequivocal expectation of the leaders of the holiness meetings—that entire sanctification was possible for any believer in the immediate present—represents a considerable shift from the understanding of this doctrine at the beginning of the century.

Through her influence in these meetings and her popular writing on the topic of holiness, Palmer outlined what became known as "altar theology." Extending the spirit of Jonathan Edwards's "immediate duty" from justification to sanctification, Palmer admonished holiness seekers to believe they could receive perfection and then to claim it—now. She urged others on to perfection, calling it the "beginning of days" for Christians rather than something a few might hope to attain toward the end of their lives. More traditional Methodists argued that simply claiming perfection in the hope of receiving it might lead to autosuggestion or self-deception and that it contradicted the Methodist doctrine of the "witness of the spirit." Yet, in the postbellum years, Palmer's ideas were so widely accepted by larger Methodist bodies that major Methodist journals promoted her book *Faith and Its Effects*. Some revivalists began to imply that without entire sanctification, one could not be saved.[16] For example, the Reverend David Kinnear maintained that "we believe that we must be entirely sanctified in this life, or never be saved."[17] The immediacy with which perfection could be attained and the urgency to attain it now led to a fervency in holiness preaching once reserved for calls to conversion.

During the Civil War, interest in the holiness movement waned. But afterward, Palmer's publications experienced an expanded circulation that paralleled a renewed interest in revivalism in general. Methodist periodicals also reported a revival taking place throughout the church.[18] Meetings based on the model of Lankford and Palmer were rapidly proliferating, mostly in urban centers of the northeast. Not only were these meetings occurring in a geographical region new to Methodism but they also were attracting people with greater resources and education.

The postwar years saw the development of yet another "special" means for the advancement of holiness. In the summer of 1866, while visiting the camp meeting in Red Bank, New Jersey, Rev. John Wood became convinced that holiness was being opposed in some camp meetings. So he suggested to Harriet E. Drake of Wilkes-Barre, Pennsylvania, that a camp meeting should be held soley to promote holiness. She offered to pay half the expenses, and the matter was brought to that tireless holiness advocate William Osborn, a minister working within the New Jersey Methodist conference. In April 1867, Osborn visited Rev. John Inskip of Green Street Methodist Episcopal in New York, and the two called a June meeting of like-minded ministers to plan just such a camp meeting. The group voted to name themselves the National Camp Meeting Association for the Promotion of Holiness and called for the first-ever "holiness" camp meeting to be at held at Vineland, New Jersey, beginning on 17 July. The ten-day meeting boasted ten thousand participants. At the close of that camp meeting, the association elected Inskip president and established itself as a permanent organization dedicated to the founding of holiness camp meetings. More than twenty thousand people attended each subsequent meeting—at Manheim, Pennsylvania, in 1868 and at Round Lake, New York, in 1869.[19]

Holiness camp meetings proved to be immensely popular throughout the northeast. Providing a familiar yet special means to pursue holiness in a church-sanctioned resort environment, they appealed particularly to the urban Methodist middle class, who were attracted to the holiness movement and who also had the recently acquired resources and time to enjoy a measure of leisure. The *Christian Advocate,* a holiness publication, records 60 meetings in the northeast in 1873, 73 in 1877, 93 in 1879, and 143 in 1889. As Charles Parker notes in his historical analysis of religious resorts in the east, "The camp meeting associations provided a Christian substitute for fashionable 'watering places.'"[20] Whether at the seaside, in the mountains, or by the lake, permanent holiness camp meetings opened popular resort environments to a generation of the Christian middle class who viewed leisure with skepticism.

As critics maintained, these holiness camp meetings were indeed different from their frontier precursors, but they were intentionally so. The holiness meetings established after Vineland drew on frontier experience: daily schedules are almost identical to those of mature frontier meetings, and the architecture is an elaboration of tents and frontier-style preacher stands. At the same time, however, these meetings introduced conceptual, environmental, and performative innovations. These modifications reflect two sources that had little effect on earlier camp meetings. First, holiness advocates brought to camp meetings their intense experience of entire sanctification as nurtured in the intimate societies of parlor gatherings. When Inskip experienced the second grace, he immediately went to Phoebe Palmer and her husband to invite them to hold special meetings for his church.[21] Later, as leader of the National Camp Meeting Association for the Promotion of Holiness, he was responsible for translating the effective means of the Tuesday society meetings—personal accountability coupled with the spiritual nurture of a small group of committed laity—into "holy" communities for the perfected. These holiness meetings became, in effect, society meetings in which the living room was expanded to encompass the entire campground. Second, the founders of permanent camp meetings heeded the progressive voices of Christian social reform in creating an environment in which leisure was also productive. A summer engaged in the recreations of camp-meeting life produced the holiness of body and mind that was necessary to sustain Christians in their work the rest of the year. Nowhere is the new camp meeting better exemplified than in the model community established by the "perfected" at Ocean Grove, New Jersey.

A New Experiment in Holiness

Shortly after nine in the evening on 31 July 1869, a few families erected ten tents in a clearing in what is now Founders' Park in Ocean Grove. They had gathered there to consider establishing a holiness camp meeting. Although some of the group had preferred to watch the moon rise over the ocean, Mrs. Thornley pressed them to hold a prayer meeting, so twenty-two people huddled by candlelight in the Thornleys' tent for the first religious service of Ocean Grove. By all accounts, the service was a success, and the assembly consecrated the land as a permanent retreat for weary urban clergy.[22]

William Osborn, with his dynamic personality and tireless enthusiasm for founding holiness camp meetings, was instrumental in establishing Ocean Grove. He was joined by a group of ministers, led by the Reverend Ellwood Stokes, who had been seeking a summer retreat for their families. Morris Daniels wrote in 1919, "The first crude thought was, Is there not, somewhere along the sea, a convenient place where a few families of like mind can pitch their tents, and for a little while in summer enjoy the sea air, bathing, fishing, etc., having such social and religious exercises intermingled as convenience and inclination might suggest?"[23] Stokes's vision was of a more informal gathering, similar to the eight or ten families who came together that first summer. He supposed the original six acres would meet their needs and "shunned" the crowds as counter to their purpose of rest and seclusion in the "desert."

The group led by Stokes apparently contemplated the notion of such a camp meeting for several years before it came to fruition. Osborn was the energetic catalyst and dreamer who tirelessly talked of a bustling camp-meeting community by the sea. After the Vineland meeting, he began to scour the New Jersey coast for a permanent site. Osborn prophesied from the beginning that the camp meeting would be a huge success and attract thousands of people. When skeptics asked him why they should invest in property in Ocean Grove, Osborn described it as "ocean and sand now; but in twenty years there will be a continuous city from Long Branch to Cape May."[24]

Osborn is said to have received the name Ocean Grove in prayer.[25] Certainly it was apt in terms of its natural surroundings; early histories record that the grounds were virtually uninhabited, a "wilderness, desert, desolation" and "so thickly vegetated that only the hardiest explorer dared enter them."[26] Daniels records that the site had been considered earlier but "because of its generally wretched unsightliness had been deemed so unpromising as to be unworthy of further consideration."[27] The committee had then selected a site near Cape May and had gone there with the intention of purchasing the land. Unable to complete the deal in one day, they had stayed the night—and changed their minds by morning: "We don't want to buy the mosquitoes."[28] Although the Ocean Grove landscape presented a greater challenge, there were no mosquitoes. When maps were later published confirming that Ocean Grove was one of the few places along the coast without these insects, the residents were further convinced that the hand of providence had guided them to this spot.

The topography, although undeveloped, was ideal for the camp meeting. The thick stand of trees provided the essential building materials and a protective canopy for the tents and the preacher's stand. In early photographs, the grounds look much like their frontier equivalent, with pruned trees still standing among the plank seating in the auditorium and throughout the tenting area. The freshwater lakes to the north and south and the ocean to the east served as natural boundaries as well as recreational areas. But before long, Ocean Grove bore little resemblance to wilderness or a grove. Osborn was exactly right.

Ocean Grove's growth was explosive, unlike the first permanent camp meeting of the northeast, Wesleyan Grove on Martha's Vineyard, which took many years to evolve from a cluster of tents to neighborhoods of permanent cottages. By contrast, the Ocean Grove Camp Meeting Association sold leases to 370 lots by the end of the first year. Three years after its founding, there were 300 permanent cottages.[29] Within a dozen years, all the streets had been graded and curbed; permanent buildings were in place; thousands made regular summer visits; and adjacent towns were taking shape. An article in the *National Repository* in 1878 charts the rapid expansion:

Figure 3. Ellwood H. Stokes, a charter member of the Ocean Grove Camp
Meeting Association and its first president, 1869–97. Reprinted from Daniels,
The Story of Ocean Grove, 15.

Figure 4. William B. Osborn, founder of Ocean Grove and a charter member of the Ocean Grove Camp Meeting Association. Reprinted from Daniels, *The Story of Ocean Grove,* 13.

It is no longer a waste and barren sand desert or tangled wildwood, but a bright and fair young city by the sea. . . . Nearly five hundred cottages, besides a score and a half of large boarding houses have been erected, while the increase is both constant and rapid. There are, also, stores, post-office, telegraph office, engine house, and a great variety of other buildings, including a fine church for the settled population.[30]

Osborn's vision and tireless energy were largely responsible for the rapid growth and success of Ocean Grove. In creating their utopian community in the wilderness, Osborn and the father/son landscape architects Frederick and Isaac Kennedy approached the natural landscape as something to be conquered and molded. Their creation of a perfect environment out of untamed wilderness mirrored the work of perfection on the raw, untamed soul. It was important philosophically and theologically for them to begin with raw terrain, outside the corrupting influences of urban industrialism and close to God's creation. But just as the newly converted soul had to be nurtured to perfection through the discipline and order of Methodism, the newly baptized soil likewise had to conform to Methodism's vision of perfected order. Ocean Grove became a canvas on which the Camp Meeting Association expressed its notion of the perfect city—perfect both in its modeling absolute order and in its ability to serve as a means of grace for citizens striving to model that perfection themselves.

In December 1869, thirteen Methodist ministers and an equal number of laymen formed the Ocean Grove Camp Meeting Association of the United Methodist Church. Many of these men had also been present for Mrs. Thornley's prayer service the previous July. The group elected Stokes as its president and appointed Osborn as superintendent to direct the daily business of the community. One of the first orders of business was to secure, from forty-four different owners, the land up to the natural boundaries. This land was then made available to lessees for their tents or summer cottages.

Tents were rented for the first two seasons from the Round Lake Association. Finding this uneconomical, the association purchased 200 tents in 1871, "but these were not sufficient to meet the demand."[31] The first permanent cottage, Pioneer Cottage, was built in 1870, and other permanent buildings—cottages, municipal buildings, boarding houses, and hotels—soon followed. The rugged terrain was cleared, leveled, and relaid in an orderly grid of streets and avenues that intersect at precise right angles. Because many trees were cut to make possible this rapid expansion, the pine grove was soon nearly gone. The community began planting trees—mostly maples—in 1879, but the grove disappeared as an architectural feature. With

Figure 5. Lake Pathway in 1870, the year after Ocean Grove's founding. Dr. Stokes and Alfred Cookman are in the left foreground. Reprinted from Daniels, *The Story of Ocean Grove*, 136.

the third auditorium, worshipers were no longer meeting under the "cathedral in the wilderness," and tall, narrow beams replaced the stately trunks of the pines.[32] Even today, Ocean Grove is a vision of order. A manicured 200-foot-wide boulevard connects the massive auditorium and beach pavilions. There are no circuitous routes, no entangling underbrush. In Ocean Grove, the "Pilgrim Pathway" is clear and direct, whether it is the pilgrimage of the soul or the street that leads from the association building to the auditorium.

A novel feature of Ocean Grove was its form of governance as stated in the charter signed with the State of New Jersey in 1870 (see appendix A). The charter established that the twenty-six trustees of the Ocean Grove Camp Meeting Association were the municipal authorities for the community. These men were to be members in good standing of the Methodist church.[33] If one of these trustees ceased to be a member of the church or engaged in conduct "incompatible with the objects and purposes of the corporation," he would be replaced. These religious leaders were responsible for making all necessary improvements, providing for mail, water, and artificial light, and hiring police to keep the laws the association passed. The peace officers were given "the same power, authority, and immunities which constables and other peace officers under the laws of this state possess or enjoy." This delineation of powers was an obvious improvement over the earlier frontier meetings, where ministers themselves often had to physically restrain or evict rowdies. But in the underlying relationship of religious to civil authority, there actually was little difference from the earlier arrangement. Law-enforcement officers sometimes assumed the responsibilities of an overburdened superintendent or moved from positions on the police force to the religious bureaucracy. Likewise, the Methodist clergy and lay leaders were directly responsible for passing ordinances that the police could enforce through fines, expulsion, or imprisonment. The Gibbonses write, "Major John C. Patterson, who was appointed chief of police in 1871, was for many years the Superintendent of Ocean Grove. Frank Tantum, his successor as chief, assisted Major Patterson by taking charge of many projects, at the same time fulfilling his duties as guardian of the law."[34]

During Ocean Grove's early years, police officers were selected from the workmen on the grounds. As the resort grew (particularly after the beginning of rail service), a more professional force was retained. In 1876, for the first time, a man was employed during the winter as a night policeman to ensure protection around the clock, throughout the year. In 1886, a "lockup" was built in the basement of the association building in order to confine "unruly people" who might have slipped through the protective watch of the gate police.

The duties of these officers apparently involved both providing general information to guests and policing the perimeter of the grounds. Daniels describes them as "walking encyclopedias and general directories for the benefit of the visitors, and guardians for the children."[35] Their chief function, of course, was to enforce the restrictions of the community and, most importantly, to guard the holy space from any contagion by the immorality and corruption of the outside world. Surrounded by water on three sides and fenced on the fourth, Ocean Grove could effectively control access to its grounds. Even when bridges were constructed across Wesley Lake, they were inscribed with plaques reading "This bridge is private property and is not dedicated to the public." A one-cent toll was charged for crossing. Posted guards at the bridge and the western gates were required to "remove nuisances of all descriptions. Among the latter class have been recorded pack-peddlers, organ-grinders, eyeglass peddlers, brass bands put off during camp-meeting, prize-package vendors, circus tumblers, noisy straw-riders, religious frauds, Punch and Judy shows, tramps, etc."[36] Annual reports recorded the police force's efficiency in protecting Ocean Grove from the "incoming lawlessness of the outside world."[37]

Although popular at seaside resorts, these buskers did not fit in a "respectable" community. They disturbed the quiet reflection of the spirit and the serious therapeutic refreshment of the body. At times, Ocean Grove was able to extend the barrier of quiet and holiness beyond its own borders, as in the early one-mile liquor law and the ban on Sunday trains at Asbury Park. Novelist Stephen Crane, acting as a correspondent from the Jersey shore, reports that the Grove policemen were even able to silence the Asbury Park Ferris wheel: "Also, residents of Ocean Grove came and said that the steam organ disturbed their pious meditations on the evils of the world. Thereupon, the minions of the law violently suppressed the wheel and its attendants."[38] Today, the community is still protected by law from vendors or buskers who might disrupt the respectable quiet of the camp meeting. In 1992, the community passed a law that forbade ice-cream, hot-dog, and other vendors from playing music or bells to attract customers, and required them to move within three minutes of serving the last customer. Even though these vendors are a staple of many seaside resorts, here they are considered a "noisy public nuisance."[39] Now, almost surrealistically, ice-cream trucks coast silently down Ocean Avenue, stopping occasionally to sell a treat but then quickly resuming their solemn, respectful course through holy ground.

The community's ordinances clearly articulated what constituted acceptable and unacceptable behavior. Today, for example, Ocean Grove's beach remains closed on Sunday until the morning worship is concluded, and several businesses likewise observe a Sabbath rest. In the late nineteenth century, rigorous blue laws were far more extensive and the topic of frequent debate. From the establishment of train service in 1875 until 1911, no Sunday trains were permitted to stop at the Ocean Grove/Asbury Park station. Merchants of neighboring Asbury Park fiercely opposed this provision, which was eventually repealed.

Despite repeated challenges, Ocean Grove was able to maintain its unique Sunday ordinance through three-quarters of the twentieth century. From its founding, the Camp Meeting Association forbade vehicular traffic of any kind between midnight Saturday and midnight Sunday. In the late nineteenth century, this meant that housewives either had to walk to Asbury Park for groceries or had to stock provisions on Saturday. Farmers coming with produce were turned away at the gate. Western Union boys walked their bicycles. With the advent of automobiles, the law was eased to allow travel for fire and medical emergencies, but otherwise there was a strict Sunday prohibition against any vehicle, moving or parked, on the streets of Ocean Grove, meaning that several thousand cars had to be moved to garages in Bradley Beach or Asbury Park before people retired on Saturday night. The Ocean Grove Camp Meeting Association strongly opposed any provision that might weaken the prohibition. Ocean Grove also successfully rebuffed a proposal to create an Ocean Avenue from Asbury Park through the Grove to Bradley Beach, contending that it would create a "race track" that would disrupt the Grove's "other-worldly stillness."[40] The streets, like all places in Ocean Grove, were sacred space. On Sundays, a respectful quiet prevailed. Not a single car was visible in the entire community. Pedestrians and children roamed freely in the streets, businesses were closed, and the beach remained deserted.

Though Ocean Grove sought to preserve the sanctity of a holy day and holy people through strict regulation of behavior and recreation, its neighbors were less inclined to do so. Asbury Park, immediately to the north, soon provided many of the activities that Ocean Grove sought to eliminate. This was not, however, the intention of its founder, James Bradley, an ardent Methodist and firm supporter of Ocean Grove. After visiting Ocean Grove in its first season, he purchased 500 acres adjacent to it to try his own experiment in moral urban planning. Asbury Park boasted the first "comprehensive" sewage system on the shore, an electric trolley, wide streets and large lots, and its own set of Sunday laws. Glenn Uminowicz suggests that Bradley tried to create the same sense of "respectability" that proved so successful in Ocean Grove by "demonstrating how both sin and sewage could be effectively discharged from a community."[41] Ocean Grove and Asbury Park used the same guidelines for regulating leisure, both insisting that their leisure activities provide rejuvenation without compromising individual morality. But Bradley hoped to create a Christian family resort that would attract a broader cross-section of the American middle class than would come to the holiness camp meeting at Ocean Grove. Realizing that not all Protestants ascribed to all the restrictions of Ocean Grove, the leaders of Asbury permitted a number of activities frowned on by the more conservative Grovers. For example, hotels freely permitted card playing and dancing. Fashionably dressed guests enjoyed strolls along the boardwalk. And the two opera houses were packed for vaudeville, minstrel shows, melodramas, and musical comedies.

Like the perimeter recreations at frontier camp meetings, the recreations just beyond the boundaries of Ocean Grove sometimes threatened to disrupt the quiet devotions of the faithful. The fairground baroque of Asbury's boardwalk carnival just across Wesley Lake from the Great Auditorium provided a stark contrast to the Grove's ascetic tents and cottages. Asbury Park had no pretenses about providing a retreat for religious renewal. Its summer guests were there to enjoy themselves, in a wholesome Christian environment, yes, but without any obligation to seek moral perfection.

Asbury Park and Ocean Grove presented two competing visions of

Figure 6. The "fairground baroque" of Asbury Park's carousel reflected the more relaxed attitude here toward popular amusements. Photograph by Troy Messenger.

Christian America's perfect leisure community. Although the landscapes of these visions differ markedly, their founders had similar roots and similar goals. In a sense, the two towns were Siamese twins under the parentage of benevolent Methodists. What was absent in one was present in the other. If the strict regulations of Ocean Grove weighed too heavily, Asbury Park offered an opportunity to step out of the holy city for a few hours. In fact, the ready access to the recreations of Asbury Park may well have made the "purity" of Ocean Grove possible. Although Wesley Lake separates the two, ferries, bridges, and the boardwalk connect them. Asbury visitors of many persuasions took advantage of the opportunities at Ocean Grove to hear some of the foremost religious and political speakers of the day. Not-quite-teetotaling Grovers could enjoy dinner with wine and an evening of dancing at the Asbury hotels without having to return to their city homes. Children of camp-meeting guests passed the summer thrilling to the carnival attractions. Today, a sign boldly proclaiming "LIQUORS" atop a building immediately across Wesley Lake is a reminder of the alternative forms of recreation that have characterized the retreats of the righteous since Cane Ridge.

Ocean Grove's ecclesiarchy did face other assaults, from within as well as without, as the community moved into the twentieth century. The Gibbonses say that the "flower . . . has been carefully cultured and kept alive

Figure 7. The "LIQUORS" sign on this Asbury Park building can easily be read from the other side of Wesley Lake in Ocean Grove. Photograph by Troy Messenger.

only after scores of figurative thorns have made their presence felt."[42] Residents and land lessees occasionally balked at the restrictive ordinances and unusual governance of the community. Adjacent towns tried several times in the early part of this century to challenge the charter and the laws that extended beyond the borders of Ocean Grove. Five times, bills were presented unsuccessfully to create a borough of Ocean Grove, which would have replaced Ocean Grove's special state charter with a more standard form of local governance. One such attempt, in 1920, was temporarily successful, but it was declared unconstitutional by the state supreme court a year later. This ruling settled the governance question for half a century, until the 1970s, when the constitutionality of the original charter would be questioned.

What began as a traffic violation eventually dismantled the century-old charter of Ocean Grove. Louis Celmer Jr. was arrested on 24 March 1976 by Ocean Grove police for drunken driving, speeding, and disregarding a traffic signal. He successfully appealed his convictions by challenging the constitutionality of the state law granting police powers to religious authorities. The New Jersey Supreme Court ruled on 21 June 1979 that the Ocean Grove Camp Meeting Association's ties with the Methodist church precluded it from exercising municipal powers. Consequently, the court ordered all municipal powers be turned over to Neptune Township. Ocean Grove was able to get two three-month stays of this order while it appealed its case to the United States Supreme Court. The federal court, however, refused to hear the appeal and let the lower court's decision stand.

On 1 January 1980, the new year marked a new era in the life of Ocean Grove, now a subdivision of Neptune Township. Nowhere else in twentieth-century America had church leaders ruled with such complete civic authority. Despite the efforts of the trustees and vocal community advocates, Ocean Grove did change dramatically after 1980. The most visible change was the dissolution of the ban on Sunday traffic, an event that symbolized for Ocean Grove residents the end of an era. The boundaries were breached. People could come and go as they pleased. Sunday streets were like the streets on any other day. The Sunday stillness was broken.

This was not, however, the end of Ocean Grove. Despite dire predictions, the community continues to thrive almost two decades later. Thousands still come for a camp-meeting revival that follows schedules created for the frontier almost two centuries ago. Hopeful tent dwellers wait up to seven years to rent one of the tents still clustered around the auditorium. Carefully maintained Victorian cottages and hotels continue to attract the urban weary. Ocean Grove is most definitely not Asbury Park or Bradley Beach. The boundaries, if not patrolled by Methodist police, are still obvious.

Community and Performance

The multiple performances of everyday life in the tents, surf, tabernacle, and streets of Ocean Grove chart a unique understanding of self and community rooted in the pietism of nineteenth-century Methodism and the liberal social-reform movements of the religious middle class. Religious history and the history of American leisure converge as Ocean Grove *performs* itself by praying and playing together.

The people and the public events they perform suggest various kinds of analysis. Church histories of the origins of camp meetings on the frontier and their evolution into the holiness camps of New England can help in placing the revivalism still evident in Ocean Grove today within the broader structure of late-nineteenth-century Methodism. But church history does not address many of the profound social and cultural questions raised by this community. Although many of the nineteenth-century moral reformers who influenced the founding of Ocean Grove were ministers or devout evangelicals, their activities in areas such as health reform, city planning, and tourism fall outside the scope of church history.

Likewise, theologians have shown the importance of understanding the role of doctrine in the changing face of nineteenth-century Methodism. Dickson Bruce Jr.'s excellent treatment of frontier camp meetings demonstrates how the theology of conversion shaped every aspect of early-nineteenth-century revivalism. In this vein, the evolving theology of perfection is instrumental in creating a need for a place like Ocean Grove. The charter, printed sermons, city ordinances, and continuing religious services outline a theology of perfection at the core of Ocean Grove. An architecture of holiness stands today as theology molded into the structures of space and time. Yet there are also dangers in trying to use belief as a sole means for understanding Ocean Grove. Although the controlling figures were within the holiness movement of the Methodist church, the citizens of Ocean Grove have always represented diverse denominational and faith backgrounds. Presbyterians, Baptists, Jews, and others willing to live according to the community's regulations were residents from the earliest years. Moreover, as Catherine Bell has shown, theological belief does not necessarily coincide with ritual or other performative behavior. She calls attention to the instability of beliefs and the multivocality of symbols to suggest that ritual activity is more like a collection of practices, ingrained in the *body* and pursued for the strategic interests of the participants.[43] For instance, while holiness theology clearly has an important place in any analysis of Ocean Grove, this theology does not completely account for why the ushers still perform their highly choreographed offertory marches. Nor does it explain how the monuments created to embody holiness in architecture become monuments for historical preservation as a "Victorian seaside resort."

Tourism, as unlikely as it may seem to students of religion, illustrates several important social dynamics behind the resort movement in camp meetings from 1835 on. Dona Brown's history of the creation of the tourist industry in New England shows how Wesleyan Grove, the first permanent camp meeting in the east, succeeded largely because it was marketed as a vacation community for religious "tourists."[44] Tourism sold intangible products like the scenery of the White Mountains and rural New England while making these products appear untainted by marketplace transactions. Brown argues that the camp meeting on Martha's Vineyard prospered not only because devout people returned out of a commitment to spiritual renewal but also because a "marketing campaign" was able to effectively sell them a "justification for leisure."[45] Glenn Uminowicz likewise shows that the "respectability" of Ocean Grove and early Asbury Park attracted vacationers who were wary of what they considered the immorality of many popular recreational sites. Quoting an early article titled "It Pays to Be Decent," Uminowicz maintains that the moral alternative offered at respectable resorts was largely responsible for ushering the religious middle class into the emerging tourist industry.[46] In fact, the Ocean Grove of today exhibits many of the trappings of a tourist attraction. The community is listed in airline magazines alongside state parks and the nightlife of urban centers.[47] The hotel and restaurant industry is the principal pillar of the economy. Many of the numerous bed-and-breakfast inns and restored Victorian hotels advertise their accommodations with little mention of the Methodist roots of the camp meeting. Ocean Grove is evolving, particularly in the post-1980 era, into a community dependent on a new generation of respectable tourists. But this approach as well, if divorced from a consideration of the unique religious character of the community, will miss the point.

Ocean Grove was "God's square mile," dedicated to a pursuit of holiness and leisure. The activities of everyday life in this carefully structured environment were performances of "holy leisure," exemplary events in the self-understanding of the community. As such, they offer essential clues for the scholar attempting to penetrate the web of intersecting powers within the community. These performances were religion, leisure, popular entertainment, and the mundane repetitive reflexes of daily life. Sometimes, they fall neatly into one of these categories. But more often, the performances of holy leisure were many things at once.

Holy leisure was a means of grace with two faces—one toward the

popular pietism of American evangelicalism and the other toward the colorful community recreations of an emerging middle class. These performances
reflected the duality of holy leisure. Through the performance of holy
leisure, Ocean Grove residents were and are able to move seamlessly between
play and devotion. At times, the performances merged, and activities became both the devotions of personal piety and community recreations.

A performance-studies approach recognizes not only that the religious
services within a camp-meeting community 125 years old are significant performances but also that the numerous informal recreations—from beach sitting to oriental bazaars—are equally revealing. All these were performances
of holiness through which the community defined and made itself.

This book does not attempt a comprehensive catalog of the myriad performances, religious and secular, commercial and noncommercial, high and
low, that have characterized the rich summers at Ocean Grove over the last
century and a quarter. Nor does it attempt an exhaustive history of this
camp-meeting community, its civic development, or even the complex issues
currently facing the community after the dissolution of its protective boundaries. Rather, this work is limited to performances rooted in the late nineteenth century during an important transitional phase in American cultural
and religious history. In this space dedicated to perfecting people in a perfect
environment, performance in time, space, and action modeled the ideal self
for Ocean Grove residents. These models were both figurative and quite
literal. Baby parades, pageants, ushers' marches, drills by the Young Rough
Riders, and the regulated order of everyday life illustrated the social structure and belief system in Ocean Grove. Residents were themselves expected
to become veritable models of the perfected Christian.

Don Handelman's paradigm for understanding public events as models
tracks the role of events such as these in the life of the community. Handelman shows that "model" events represent the whole in microcosm. They are
teleological in suggesting an appropriate change and in monitoring "feedback" to attempt to effect that change. Rites of passage, for example, are
models. In the camp meeting, the evangelistic preaching service that led a
person to a "salvation experience" worked as a model. The desired outcome
of the event—that is, changing a person from not being a Christian to being
a Christian—was both modeled and actually accomplished through the
model. Moreover, this change on the individual level modeled the intention
of the community as a whole—the teleological movement toward a converted people.[48] At Ocean Grove, a parachurch holiness movement converged
with the nascent middle-class tourist industry and utopian dreams of liberal
social planners. The models spawned in this environment defined what it

meant to be a "holy" person in a quickly changing American society. These performances were a "means of grace" for holiness people. They were not neutral. They were not mere entertainment. They helped create certain kinds of people. They were and are the tools by which the residents of Ocean Grove continue to negotiate the reality of holiness. The people molded by these performances live on in Ocean Grove. Some come back generation after generation for a summer in a two-room family tent. Some lie on the beach with their bikini tops untied. Some do both.

2

HOLY RHYTHMS

They arrive on Memorial Day weekend. Taking advantage of the three-day holiday, tenters move their summer belongings into the cluster of closely spaced wood-frame-and-canvas tents hugging the perimeter of the auditorium. Each family adds a special touch to make it home. Many take advantage of the Ladies Auxiliary to the Auditorium Ushers' plant sale. Porches sprout flags, wind chimes, hand-painted signs, and rocking chairs. The interiors are domesticated with small, but tasteful, furniture carefully placed in the combination living/dining/bedrooms. On Sunday, the returnees are welcomed by a special service at St. Paul's Methodist Church. On Monday, they fill the sidewalks of Main Avenue for the annual Memorial Day parade. Although some of the tenters must return to the city for a few weeks while children finish spring terms and parents wait for vacation time, Ocean Grove has come to life. What were dormant rows of plain wooden boxes and empty tent frames have become summer homes for late-twentieth-century holiness seekers.

Revivalists have always been careful to distinguish camp meeting from the quotidian, both sacred and profane. The events that comprise the camp-meeting experience from the early nineteenth century to the present are as different from ordinary church as they are from everyday domesticity and labor. The success of this movement in American Methodism can be attributed largely to the ability of the camp meeting to articulate a unique temporal and spatial order with clearly marked boundaries. There was no mistaking the several days of around-the-clock preaching, praying, and exhorting in the woods with the rhythms of daily life and work on a frontier farm. Likewise, the gates, chains, and moats around Ocean Grove marked a threshold containing sacred play. This careful demarcation of time and space defined a stage on which the performances of holy leisure could be played and through which these events could be known as means of grace. The defining attribute of the camp meeting at Ocean Grove was and is the unique way people here act together to model perfection. At Ocean Grove, the architecture of holiness—that is, the highly organized time and space—structures people and their action.

Memorial Day weekend marks an unmistakable beginning at Ocean Grove. Likewise, the march around the grounds on Labor Day effectively signals the end of the camp-meeting season. Though people come and go throughout the summer, there is never a question about when camp meeting occurs. Drawing on the lessons of a half-century of camp-meeting experience, the founders of Ocean Grove developed an ordering of time that maintained the spiritual rigor of nonpermanent revivals but also allowed ordered, regular rest and recreation. Holy leisure meant there was plenty of time for devotion and play. It also meant that the two could often happen simultaneously.

When the camp-meeting phenomenon swept rural America in the first years of the nineteenth century, the frontier families who packed up to spend a week in the woods did not know the luxury of family vacations. Driven by both economic necessity and a Protestant work ethic that deplored the frivolities of unproductive time, most early participants in camp meetings had rarely experienced such an extended time away from the rhythms of daily work. Ted Ownby's study of recreation in the rural areas of the south where frontier meetings flourished demonstrates that, in the nineteenth century, leisure activities were primarily nonprofessional and enjoyed around the edges of one's other duties.[1] Hunting, barn-raisings, drinking, and visiting allowed some diversion but did not disrupt the daily schedules of home and work.

Camp meetings, on the other hand, broke the pattern of hard work and informal leisure by imposing a wholly different temporal order. The Reverend Barlow Weed Gorham, author of the most popular manual for camp meetings, suggested that the events should be long enough to thoroughly disengage campers from secular concerns but not so long as to wear out the laborers who must immediately return to fields and factories.[2] The five to eight days that Gorham recommended were standard throughout the nineteenth century.

By all accounts, people disregarded their usual rhythms of daily life during a camp meeting. The earliest camp meetings were a continuous festival of activity, often extending through the night. As one preacher finished, the crowd surged toward another. Because of the huge masses of people, several preachers often spoke simultaneously, with the loudest and most engaging drawing the largest crowd. Some people labored in prayer throughout the night. Preachers, lay exhorters, and members of the congregation each made their own times improvisationally "as led by the spirit" within the carnival-like freedom of the sacred time. Members of the congregation spontaneously broke into hymn singing or "exercises." Preachers might stop a sermon and call for prayer for someone on the mourners' bench.

This amorphous festival temporality underscored the difference between camp-meeting and ordinary time by disrupting linear profane time with numerous simultaneous and spontaneous events. Pulled in many directions at once, the camper experienced disorientation. And this *dis*-orienting from ordinary time further distinguished the temporal structure of early camp meetings as out of the ordinary, as a sacred festival time. Brooks McNamara records a similar disorientation in the festive atmosphere of the carnival, where there is no official beginning or end. Everything happens at once. The spectator must not only choose a sequence through the events but must also contend with simultaneous multiple performances. McNamara suggests that carnival showmen use this disorientation to draw the spectator through the environment from one attraction to another.[3] In a similar fashion, participants at the early camp meetings were pulled from one event to another by the flow of emotional and religious energy through the meeting in response to preaching, singing, and religious exercises. As in the carnival, the leaders tried to draw people in from the perimeter toward the most significant activities.

The dramatic disruption of everyday routine with a weeklong period in which people were free to choose their own times to sing, pray, listen, eat, sleep, and visit had implications for leisure as well as religion. Even in these earliest years, the sacred and recreational aspects of camp meetings always coexisted. Whether or not it was intended by the organizers, the frontier camp meeting, being the only break in a continuous flow of secular time, quickly became a family vacation.[4] Although one parent or the other may have attended camp meetings alone, coming and going as schedules permitted, entire families, including young children, also attended for several days at a time.[5] Because domestic responsibilities were minimal during the camp period and because attendance at the religious activities depended upon the spontaneity of the individual, many people took advantage of this "time out of time" to enjoy the company of others in what became a vacation time for whole communities.

Young people often courted one another during camp meetings.[6] The following excerpt from a letter suggests that young people attended several camp meetings to be "in fashion":

> You will recollect that this is the season of the year for Campmeetings in this country and as everybody attends them I cannot be out of fashion. I have lately been at four first Baptist next Methodist third Prebeterian and last Christian. You would have been amused at the different characters that attend those big meetings. Some daddy beans strutting and whirling about with great self importance and our sects to equal them.[7]

As this quotation illustrates, ritual and play coexisted at frontier camp meetings. Some people obviously came to enjoy a holiday in the company of neighbors, while others attached greater importance to the religious activities. Many, however, seem to have come for *both* leisure and holiness, even when these two types of activities were distinct and contradictory.

For example, the male recreations that were usually available at the margins of the work day were also available at the margins of the camp meeting. Participants had only to step into the woods to enjoy a shot of whiskey, a hearty brawl, and the pleasures of the opposite sex. Yet even beyond the perimeter, people might not escape the effects of the camp meeting. Men around the whiskey barrel might suddenly succumb to ecstatic movements of the body called "jerks" or "slain in the spirit." At other times, the brawling in the woods threatened to disrupt the sacred proceedings. Although constables were appointed to keep order, it was often the preacher who had to keep the drinking, brawling, and merrymaking from interfering with the saving of souls. In the 1860s, Rev. William George Matton wrote of one such encounter:

> I was duly qualified as a special constable, and went at once, to the scene of the tumult, and elbowing my way into the midst, which my character as a preacher made comparatively easy, I took each of the culprits by the arm, and told them I had authority, to take them before the magistrate.[8]

The disorderliness of piety and recreation in these early meetings was partly a result of the loose temporal order of camp-meeting time. The temporal boundaries of camp meetings created a free space divorced from everyday schedules that permitted participants to devise their own patterns of worship and sociability. This dynamism no doubt was a large factor in the success of the initial camp meetings, but it was also a threat to Methodist respectability.

Methodists began the century outside the cultural and religious mainstream and by the end of the century were at its center.[9] Randall Balmer notes that the institutionalization of the camp meeting came at a period when Methodists "were eager to shed their image as an insurgent denomination confined predominantly to the frontier."[10] By midcentury, Methodist leaders had successfully moderated both the sacred and play elements of camp meetings by imposing a carefully constructed ordering of camp-meeting time. Roger Robins charts a parallel growth of both the numbers of Methodists and their "pilgrimage to respectability."[11] While frontier revivalism was extremely successful in funneling vast numbers of the unchurched into Methodist churches, the resultant denominational bureaucracy moved increasingly away from the uncontrolled rowdiness of the woods toward the more "civilized" semipermanent and permanent camp meetings.

The spontaneity and improvisation of the first meetings were replaced with the rigid standardization of every aspect of camp meeting and control of all intemperate behavior, religious and social. Preachers no longer vied with each other for the attention of the crowds. There were set times for each speaker, as well as times when families might gather for a meal or private prayer. The camp-meeting manuals published around 1850 illustrate the maturing of the camp-meeting form.[12] Gorham's manual outlines the routinization of the daily schedule, punctuated by trumpet blasts to move the crowds from one event to the next:

5:00	Rise
6:30–7:30	Family prayer and breakfast
8:30	General prayer meeting at altar
10:30	Preaching and prayer meeting to noon
12:30	Lunch
2:00 or 2:30	Preaching followed by prayer at altar until 5:00
6:00	Tea
7:30	Preaching and prayer until 9:00 or 10:00
10:00	Visitors required to leave and lights out[13]

Although these schedules left less time for visits to the whiskey seller, camp meetings nevertheless remained a form of recreation. Yet respectability meant that the recreational aspect of the camp, if it was to survive, had to become part of holy work. Even in these "new style" camp meetings, large crowds took a holiday from their work and enjoyed the company of distant neighbors for perhaps the only time that year. Parker's analysis of the transformation of camp meetings from the frontier to the seaside demonstrates that although the improvisational elements were controlled through the imposition of a rigorous schedule of religious activities, the participants still enjoyed the meetings as leisure.

> Wesleyan asceticism demanded a negative appraisal of idle pastimes. Having banished secular levity, however, Methodists freed themselves to enjoy holy levity, a sacred holiday. The social side of camp meeting, now translated into the language of revival and rigorously subordinated to spiritual objectives, made sacred work out of social play. "Idle recreation" became "sweet Christian Conference," and the campground became sanctified recreational space.[14]

One of the earliest examples of this transformation of a meeting site to a "sanctified recreational space" occurred on Martha's Vineyard at Wesleyan Grove. Unlike the rural camp meetings, which were scheduled either early in the summer after planting season (20 June–15 July) or before harvest (20 August–15 September), this version of the camp meeting took advantage of a new form of leisure time popular with the emerging religious middle class—the vacation. Founded in 1835, Wesleyan Grove was in the vanguard of Methodist cultural change. Parker suggests that the order established in this community "reflected and anticipated the refined Methodism that would assume leadership in the denomination's hierarchy and evoke genteel theologies."[15]

By the 1850s, crowds were coming two weeks early to "rusticate."[16] Although the camp meeting proper lasted ten days, most people came for an extended stay. Because the only means of access was by ferry, the kind of casual attendance in evidence on the frontier was no longer possible. Robins rightly notes, "One form of money required at Wesleyan Grove was time."[17] Some writers bemoaned the increasing prominence of leisure time at Wesleyan Grove. One guest, writing in 1866, complained that "instead of . . . the work of grace and goodness, we hear the merry jest and see the rallying around the croquet ground."[18] At the same time, however, the socially concerned religious leaders of the mid-nineteenth century were extolling the practice of summer vacations.[19] Henry Ward Beecher wrote extensively on the moral and religious benefits of vacations for urban professionals, proclaiming they were essential to the health of city dwellers.

In 1869, when William Osborn and his fellow ministers were searching for an appropriate site for a camp meeting, it was understood that families would come to the new place as much for rest and recreation as for religious services. Ocean Grove was heir both to the highly structured camp meetings of a mature Methodism and to the nearby resorts of the nascent seaside leisure industry. Osborn, echoing Beecher, wanted to provide ministers from the cities with a time and space to rejuvenate themselves before returning to their ministries. Time away from the increasingly demanding urban schedules was as important as time for revival. The theology of renewal was beginning to more explicitly equate time itself as a means of grace. In contrast to Wesleyan Grove of 1850, the founders of Ocean Grove did not have to defend the practice of spending time at the camp-meeting grounds before and after the centerpiece revival. Osborn imagined from the beginning a community in residence for the entire summer. As his paper proclaims in 1875, "All hail *religion, recreation, rest!*"[20]

The daily schedule, even outside the ten days specifically designated as the camp meeting, looked remarkably like the schedule proposed in Gorham's manual for a camp meeting. Parker describes a day in Ocean Grove:

> Ten to fifteen services of various types occurred throughout the day, beginning at five or five-thirty in the morning and lasting until ten or ten-thirty at night. Prayer meetings, experience meetings, love-feasts, communion services all might be held, some consecutively, and some simultaneously.[21]

Following is a schedule from 1 July 1883 as reported in the *Ocean Grove Record:*

9:00	Mr. and Mrs. Palmer's bible class
10:30	Auditorium service
Afternoon	Bible class
Early tea	
6:00	Surf meeting
Evening	Service in auditorium[22]

Judging from other contemporary accounts, there was still ample time either before or after these events or instead of them to enjoy the recreational opportunities of the Grove. When the leaders faced criticism that the "camp-meeting degenerates into a scene of recreation, with a few religious exercises for a pasttime," they responded that most city dwellers took a summer rural retreat and that in "most places Satan goes along." Here, they said, it was possible to "rest the body and feast the soul at the same time."[23]

The rhythms of "religion, recreation, and rest" varied throughout the summer at Ocean Grove. Not everyone arrived at the same time or stayed for the same period. But the largest crowds and the greatest concentration of activities have always occurred during the eight to ten days of camp meeting per se. In the early years, winter was a period of relative dormancy, and residents were required to obtain special permits to stay past the close of the season; the tents and summer cottages were not built to weather the harsh New Jersey winters. Even today, a visit to Ocean Grove in February will find many of the hotels closed, shops open on limited schedules, cottages empty, and the tents removed.

During the "season" at Ocean Grove—Memorial Day to Labor Day—there was a mixture of religious and recreational offerings. Each day was ordered by the pattern of daily meetings, trips to the beach, devotions, and community recreations. As the summer progressed, attendance gradually rose and so did the frequency of events. By the beginning of July, there was always a crowd on hand for Independence Day celebrations. Residency peaked in late July through August, when the camp meeting and most of the community activities were planned. Some years, tens of thousands of people would gather in the auditorium, on the beach, or along the banks of Wesley Lake for late-summer events. During Carnival Week, which was immediately before the beginning of the revival, huge crowds gathered for festive performances that marked the end of the leisure season. Featuring events like a procession of illuminated boats, the Fairyland Pageant, the Ushers' Show, and the Asbury Baby Parade, Carnival Week festivities, characterized by nonreligious themes, boasted the largest attendance of any events at Ocean Grove. When the revival week began, the community maintained this level of activity, but now the events were myriad services and holiness meetings. These meetings reached a high point on the penultimate day of the meeting. The closing day of the camp-meeting week—on Labor Day until the middle of this century—was more subdued. The period dominated by recreation and nonreligious pageants was clearly divided from camp-meeting week; Carnival Week and camp-meeting week were two movements in one ritual whole that allowed summer guests to use recreation and religion in sequence to model holiness.

This slowly moving temporal arch shaped the lives of the summer guests who came to act out their holy leisure under it. The time summer residents spent at Ocean Grove was clearly separate from everyday time. As strictly ordered as camp time might appear, it still had the quality of festival time. The absence of domestic and work responsibilities created a vacuum that summer residents filled with a plethora of religious and recreational possibilities. As on the frontier, leaders tried to steer people toward the core activities such as those listed on the above schedule. There were always other options, however, including leisure. The careful structure of camp-meeting time went beyond ordering the activities of daily life. Camp-meeting attendees have often described themselves as participating in pivotal faith events that transcended ordinary time, that were oriented in a time of faith, or mythic time. Despite the vast differences between the daily schedules of the raucous frontier meetings and those of the genteel family resorts of the Victorian era, participants at both types of camp meetings understood the connection between what they were doing and events associated with biblical times.

The belief that camp meetings participated in mythic time changed little from the days of Cane Ridge to Ocean Grove. Mircea Eliade claims that in an effort to reintegrate a primordial experience, religious people ritually reenact mythical experiences of the past. He says that a "festival always takes place in the original time."[24] When Methodists write about their camp meetings, they convey a sense of participation in another time—either a biblical time in the *past,* when God was visibly present with a separated, chosen people, or a time of the *future,* when God will return and reign on earth with the faithful few. Referred to as the Feast of Booths, a wilderness rest with Jesus, the Millennium, or Sabbath, camp-meeting time was a return to a time when God was physically present, creatively molding people and the world.

The most-often cited model, the Jewish Feast of Booths/Tabernacles (Succoth), required the Israelites to live in booths for one week every year.[25] This annual holiday recalls the Hebrews' exodus from Egypt; as the chosen people of God wandered through the desert toward the promised land, God appeared to them as a cloud by day and a pillar of fire by night. The biblical account of this passage paints it as a period of transformation. God was personally reshaping a people for forty years so they could emerge ready to form a nation in Palestine. While in the wilderness, the people lived in temporary dwellings—tents and booths—that could be easily dismantled when they had to move. They ate manna that was provided daily by divine miracle. The festival recalls this period of dependence and transformation for the Jewish people.

Camp-meeting apologists like Gorham used this model to suggest that God also called Christians to an annual wilderness meeting:

> Here then, we have by express institution of God, a religious convocation, identical with a modern Camp Meeting in its principle or characteristic fact, namely, that the people were to leave their dwelling-houses and live in tents during the meeting.[26]

By observing the time of tent dwelling, campers connected themselves mythically to biblical time, and claimed contemporaneity with God as God was preparing a selected group of people for a promised paradise. Even when camp meetings began to take the form of summer retreats that extended well beyond the prescribed eight-day celebration, leaders continued to cite this paradigmatic festival. Wesleyan Grove historian Hebron Vincent wrote at midcentury, "Tired nature occasionally seeks repose from the toil and strife of business. The ancient Jewish festivals were no less the means of restoring the social and intellectual equilibrium, than of promoting religious sentiment and devotional feeling."[27]

In the New Testament, the wilderness image returns with Jesus' own frequent withdrawals to the desert. According to the gospel account, after his baptism, Jesus spent forty days fasting in the wilderness in preparation for the beginning of his earthly ministry.[28] Later, he frequently withdrew from the crowds for periods of prayer and rest.[29] Gorham and other writers cited this New Testament evidence to provide a specifically Christian justification and interpretation of the Jewish festival.[30] The *Ocean Grove Record* reminded its readers of the "Savior's instruction" to "come apart into a desert place and rest awhile."[31] When coupled with the recurrent images of camp meeting as Succoth, the wilderness experience assumes a heightened sacredness. Campers are at once contemporaneous with *both* the God of the Hebrew exodus and with the first-century Jesus. In mythic time, the biblical wilderness images become one past where God as both Creator and Son was physically present.

The mythic order of time at Ocean Grove not only linked participants to a time of beginnings but it also made present a promised future when Christ would once again dwell on earth with his people. In the language of nineteenth-century evangelicalism, the millennium was a near and present reality. The earth and its people—or, more specifically, America and evangelical Christians—were preparing to receive the predicted thousand-year reign of Christ on earth. In biblical and devotional literature, the millennium was characterized as a period of joy, rest from labors, and unhindered access to the presence of the Christ. Overwhelmed with the sights, sounds, and religious energy of the early camp meetings, it was not hard for the participants to believe they were at the threshold of the millennium. Thomas Owen wrote in 1800 that "singing, Preaching Praying & Rejoicing from place to place both night & day several times in a week God is working wonders. There the Millennium is certainly about to commence."[32] Three-quarters of a century later, an article in the *Ocean Grove Record* claimed that the Grove's welcome of diverse people "antedated the coming millennium."[33]

In the time between these two statements, the interest in eschatological theologies had increased significantly within evangelical circles, particularly among holiness leaders. By the last quarter of the century, the "world-rejection" that Bruce describes as being at the "heart of frontier conversion experiences" had given way to a postmillennialism that maintained that this

HOLY RHYTHMS — 39

world would be perfected for the millennial reign of God on earth.[34] The perfection of individuals, which was the core of holiness theology, was indeed a precondition to this coming time of societal perfection. Furthermore, individual perfection had global temporal implications. Kenneth Brown has documented this interplay between the theologies of perfection and eschatology: "When the holiness advocates spoke of 'entire sanctification,' . . . in a very real way they spoke eschatologically and to miss that point is to fail to understand a major part of holiness theology."[35] Despite the horrific experience of the Civil War, holiness advocates were able to proclaim that not only individuals but also the entire world was perched on the edge of perfection. Brown continues, "One thing is certain, out of the ashes of war came a renewed emphasis, a cleansed emphasis, that the dawn of the millennial day was about to begin, and with the holiness advocates this new emphasis came through the proclamation of a cleansing theology, the theology of holiness."[36]

Personal perfection in holiness was a sign that the millennium was at hand. Holiness-camp-meeting leaders believed they could literally bring in the time of perfection by becoming perfect people in a perfect place. Brown quotes a resident of Ocean Grove to illustrate this connection between personal holiness, millennial time, and holy place:

> In the summer of 1871, Alfred Cookman and his wife were sitting in front of their cottage at Ocean Grove. Brother Cookman, wearied with his journey to Urbana, was sweetly resting at his summer home on the margin of Wesley Lake. We were invited to a seat; and, during the conversation that followed, Mrs. Cookman, in answer to some remark, said, "Oh, the millennium will take place before that." Turning to Brother Cookman, I observed, "Some ministers talk a great deal about the millennium, and of its rapid approach, while others give the subject no attention. What do you think about it, Brother Cookman?" His face lit up with one of those sweet smiles his friends enjoyed so much, and, placing his hand on his heart, replied, "Brother, the millennium is now: it is in this poor heart."[37]

For Alfred Cookman, the summer evening in Ocean Grove was the onset of the millennium. Chronological time stood still while the heart of the perfected dwelt in a timeless millennium that was both future and present.

Participation in a timeless time out of time meant the cessation of utilitarian time, stopping the clock of minutes and hours. Whether in the biblical wilderness or around the throne of God, the experience of holiness was pursued through purposeful resting—holiness through leisure.

In Jewish and Christian traditions, all periods of rest derive from the primordial rest of the Creator on the seventh day of creation. Eviatar

Zerubavel describes how people use these times of resting to identify themselves ritually with the God who rested. "The most conspicuous ritual act of imitating God and reactualizing the act of Creation is probably the Sabbath rest. . . . In other words, the Sabbath rest is a ritual act whose main function is to symbolically reactualize God's rest following the Creation of the World."[38] Zerubavel shows that, for Jews, the strictness with which the Sabbath is observed is not a matter of prohibition but a matter of distinguishing Sabbath time (and thus Sabbath people) from other time and other people.[39] Similarly, Ted Ownby records that nineteenth-century evangelicals prepared for the eternal Sabbath rest by observing quiet Sabbath days each Sunday.[40]

The summer rest at Ocean Grove modeled a Sabbath rest that was longer than a day—a foretaste of the coming perfection when every day would be Sabbath. Coming to Ocean Grove, where time was always like Sabbath time, allowed summer guests to take an extended Sabbath from city life and work. As Ownby has shown, Sabbath was the time reserved for attention to matters of the soul, and levity and self-indulgence were decidedly not Sabbath behavior.[41] People were able to rest from their usual occupations, and many other activities were prohibited as well. Self-denial as a means of personal piety was a common theme throughout nineteenth-century evangelicalism. John Wesley himself exhorted his followers to lead model lives of personal piety through a self-denial that forbade

> taking the name of God in vain; profaning the day of the Lord, either by doing ordinary work thereon, or by buying or selling; drunkenness, buying or selling spirituous liquors, or drinking them, unless in cases of extreme necessity; fighting, quarreling, brawling; going to law; returning evil for evil, or railing for railing, the using many words in buying or selling; the buying or selling uncustomed goods; the giving or taking things on usury; uncharitable or unprofitable conversation; doing to others as we would not they should do unto us; doing what we know is not for the glory of God, as the putting on of gold or costly apparel; the taking such diversions as cannot be used in the name of the Lord Jesus, the singing those songs or reading those books which do not tend to the knowledge or love of God; softness and needless self-indulgence; laying up treasure upon earth.[42]

At Ocean Grove, similar prohibitions were in effect throughout the summer, and it was illegal to drink or sell alcoholic beverages, to dance, to sell cigarettes, or to fight. For these infractions, an Ocean Grove guest could land in the campground jail. It was also not permitted to enjoy "softness and needless self-indulgence," not because of city ordinances or the watchful eye of municipal authorities but because holy leisure as it was performed by community residents did not sanction such things. Summer at Ocean Grove was an extended Sabbath, a time of communion with God, a prelude to the eternal rest. This meant modeling Sabbath behavior throughout the summer, because holy leisure was the performance of holy time.

If the Sabbath at Ocean Grove lasted an entire summer, Sundays marked the holiest of holies within the sacred time of camp meeting. Although Ocean Grove prohibited numerous activities and thus distinguished the entire summer as a special holy time, the community was particularly vigilant in preserving the sanctity of the Sunday quiet. Daniels advertises that "to the thoughtful people the Sabbath quiet is one of the chief attractions of Ocean Grove."[43] Although driving is now permitted on Sunday, the beach is still closed on Sunday morning. The performance of Sunday as a particularly sacred time within a summer of holy time was a key in establishing Ocean Grove's identity. As if to emphasize this statement of identity, the Sunday of camp-meeting week was subject to even more restrictions. Because even the huge Great Auditorium could not accommodate everyone who wanted to attend services on this day, Ocean Grove residents received "cards of admission," while people from neighboring towns were prohibited from entering.[44]

People left cluttered homes and hectic schedules to come to the Grove and enter a sacred time of re-formation when they could touch both the sacred beginnings and sacred end of time. In contrast to the earliest frontier camp meetings, time was highly ordered. An important component of this experience was the structuring of both piety and leisure. The structure of holy time was one of several models in Ocean Grove that made holiness visible, a tangible reality, in the activities of everyday life. By moving people not only to see holiness but also to pray and play in holy rhythms closer to the ideals of Wesleyan perfection, the temporal order of Ocean Grove was also a means of grace.

3

HOLY SPACE

Ocean Grove is a city that is at once an earthly and a heavenly home, a bridge between the everyday world of the city and the millennial new Jerusalem. Carved out of the "wilderness" in the utopian spirit of the age, Ocean Grove modeled an entire town on a vision of personal and community holiness. In the postmillennial fervor of the age, the founders of this and other religious communities felt they might actually be building the promised perfect city to come. Although this model of perfection relied on close physical contact with the natural world, it was also understood to be an idealized city with private dwellings, generous boulevards, manicured parks, and cavernous meeting halls for worship. In the hymns and writings of late-nineteenth-century evangelicalism, presence with God in the time to come is expressed not as a return to a natural state modeled on the Garden of Eden but, rather, as finding the perfect home in a city filled with God's people.

> There's a land that is fairer than day,
>   And by faith we can see it afar;
> For the Father waits over the way,
>   To prepare us a dwelling-place there.
>
> In the sweet by-and-by,
>   We shall meet on that beautiful shore;
> In the sweet by-and-by,
>   We shall meet on that beautiful shore. (*VOP,* 956)[1]

43

In Ocean Grove, a dwelling place on that beautiful shore modeled holiness.

With nothing more than a clearing in the woods, crude canvas or board shelters, planks to sit on, and raised platforms for the speakers, early revivalists created a remarkable architectural space to accommodate an equally extraordinary performance of Methodist self-identity. Robins argues that the "vernacular landscape" of camp meetings, spare as it was, nonetheless "was a profoundly revealing exercise in symbolic architecture. It was Methodism carving its initials on the face of the earth."[2] The Methodists and other evangelicals who created camp-meeting architecture were cultural and spiritual heirs to the Reformation's architectural asceticism. In this tradition, church leaders rejected baroque ornamentation for a simplicity that is evident in early American meeting-house architecture. John Jackson reminds us that the term *meeting house* and the subsequent use of *camp meeting* instead of *church* to designate the spaces for religious events are based on the belief that "no place is in itself especially sacred; only its use is sacred."[3] Already in colonial America, the traditional notion of space as inherently sacred was waning; replacing it was the notion that the actions of a sacred people—that is, their *meeting*—was what made a space hallowed.

Yet it was impossible to erase the profound effects of sacred space, even in the most minimalist examples issuing from Reformed theology. The clearing in the woods did not eliminate religious architecture any more than did the Ocean Grove tent. The camp-meeting clearing and the Ocean Grove tent were prime examples of Methodist sacred architecture, designed to facilitate particular performances of holiness for two centuries of camp-meeting participants.

Influencing the design of camp-meeting architecture was a desire to create a space where the Holy Spirit had uninterrupted freedom to work in the heart of every participant. To worship in "spirit and truth" meant doing so in a space devoid of visual distractions that might turn one away from the movement of the Holy Spirit. Even at the earliest camp meetings, the architecture of tents, brush arbors, and temporary cottages was an essential feature of the rituals performed there. Throughout the camp-meeting movement, from the woods to the seaside, the landscape functioned as a setting for sacred performances, a stage on which conversion or sanctification rituals were to be played. This architecture was not, however, a static backdrop to the performance of faith. The space of camp meeting, like the time, created the possibility for particular actions and, thus, became itself a means of grace.

Jackson correctly notes that the move to outdoor spaces indicated "a rejection of traditional space" identified with a "social order" in which many of the participants held the least desirable locations.[4] Indeed, implicit in the move out of the church and civic centers is a rejection of the order imposed by those institutions. Yet as Methodists moved from a position outside the social mainstream to a reforming position within that mainstream, they simultaneously moved from transient constructions in the woods to permanent camp-meeting communities. Paralleling the move from disorderly time to highly ordered schedules, permanent camp-meeting architecture restored a degree of formalism and hierarchy to the unruly assemblages. A circle enclosing a performance space with constantly moving preachers and congregants was replaced at Ocean Grove by streets at right angles and a massive ten-thousand-seat auditorium with fixed seating and podium. The evolution from disorder to order, in space as in time, was an exercise in model building.

Ocean Grove's architecture of holiness modeled perfection in three ways. First, by using the structures associated with pilgrimage, the architecture extended the mythic link already established through camp-meeting time to places of extraordinary meeting between the human and the divine. Second, the physical structures and their environment presented a visible picture of the perfect order, tidiness, economy, and beauty of the heavenly home to come. And third, the architecture structured action in a way that facilitated the performance of a particular notion of holiness. For example, tents connected the community to the wilderness meeting with God; their perfect rows of translucent walls allowed campers a foretaste of the heavenly city lit from within by the glory of God; and the proximity of their walls to adjacent tents required the kind of accountability required by Wesleyan societies. In each of these ways, the community modeled perfection. Given different architecture, these performances—and perfection itself—would be different.

The natural environment was integral to this construction of space. A stand of trees, a grove, supplied building material and connected the site mythically to the place of holy meeting.[5] The grove linked the camp-meeting participants to the Jewish *succa*, or wilderness booth. Worshiping under a brush arbor, campers marked themselves as pilgrims, temporary residents moving mythically with the ancient Israelites from one home to the next. In this case, of course, it was a pilgrimage between Philadelphia or New York and the new Jerusalem, and the spiritual path through the wilderness was the undeveloped land of the nineteenth-century Jersey shore.

The first auditorium at Ocean Grove maintained the traditional brush-arbor architecture essential to this mythology. Porous branches blocked direct sunlight but not rain from the congregants, who sat on crude plank benches. Even as the auditorium increased in size, it retained the essence of this architectural style. The many doors and windows, left open during

Figure 8. The first auditorium was very similar to frontier encampments, with plank seating, a covered preaching platform, and trees for shade. Reprinted from Daniels, *The Story of Ocean Grove,* 56.

summer events, give the impression that the architecture was more covering than enclosure, an extension of the wilderness arbor and not yet a church.

Gorham argued that the camp-meeting structures should evoke the biblical pilgrimage of the Hebrews. Besides the arbor and preaching stand, he maintained that tents were an essential feature in re-creating the mythical stage on which the camp-meeting ritual was to be played. "Dwelling in the goodly tents of Jacob," campers performed a Christianized Succoth. Gorham's manual provided detailed instructions for constructing family tents as well

Figure 9. Approximately 100 family tents are still clustered around the auditorium in Ocean Grove today. Because the tent on the corner has not yet been occupied for the summer, a striped porch awning hangs over the front door. Porches of occupied tents generally contain chairs so residents can sit and chat with their neighbors. Photograph by Troy Messenger.

as the other camp-meeting structures. He suggested that for a family of six to eight, the tent should be twelve feet square, with a frame of three posts to a side and covered with forty feet of "factory cloth." He decried the practice of makeshift wooden cabins, which he said looked like Irish "shanties" and were dark, not waterproof, and more expensive to construct.[6] Gorham may also have disliked wooden tents because they did not as effectively model ancient pilgrimage for American evangelicals.

Family tents, the first form of architecture in Ocean Grove and still popular today, could be leased inexpensively through the Camp Meeting Association; this allowed people of even modest means to spend a week or two at the shore. For the families who have passed their tent leases from generation to generation, tent dwelling epitomizes the camp-meeting experience.

A quite different situation on Martha's Vineyard illustrates the distinctive role of architecture in each place within the camp-meeting experience. Wesleyan Grove began much like a frontier camp meeting. In 1835, the ground was cleared of underbrush, and the people erected on a half-acre a simple wooden preacher's "tent," a pulpit, temporary altar, backless benches, and nine society tents.[7] The steady growth through the first two decades of this camp meeting was accommodated solely through the addition of tents. In 1842, almost 1,200 people were staying in 40 tents; by 1851, there were 100 tents; and by 1855, there were 150 family tents and 50 society tents.[8]

With the increasing formalization of the landscape, the lengthening stays, the repeat visits by faithful summer guests, and the growing popularity of the retreat, a new architectural form—the campground cottage—was adopted on Martha's Vineyard in the 1860s. The cottage met the needs of guests returning to the meeting grounds year after year. It offered the convenience of a permanent structure, greater protection from the elements, and more of the comforts of home. The wooden cottages quickly surpassed tents in popularity at Wesleyan Grove and eventually replaced the entire tent community. In 1868, the year before Ocean Grove was founded, there were 250 cottages and 300 tents. Soon, only the Fourth Street tents remained as something of a "pre-cottage" historic district; the residents of this street were reputed to be the most pleasant because they lived in "primitive camp-meeting architecture." By 1914, only one tent remained on the grounds.[9]

Ocean Grove, on the other hand, moved from an exclusively tent community almost immediately to a combination of cottages and tents, but a committed neighborhood of tent residents remains to this day. Economics was probably a factor in the early decades, while the unique lifestyle provided by the tent village is no doubt why it continues to exist. Because of the greater expense involved in reaching Martha's Vineyard, Wesleyan Grove attracted more well-heeled guests, who selected the more expensive cottages for their increased comfort. Ocean Grove, however, was accessible by rail and stage from Philadelphia and New York City for a round-trip fare of five dollars. The *Ocean Grove Record* quotes Olive Logan of *Harper's* in 1876: "It is a sort of poor man's paradise, though there are rich people there; but even the rich dwell in modest cottages, while those who must practice a close economy live in tents or in cheaply constructed cabins in the woods."[10] Uminowicz, on the other hand, observes that the "core clientele for Ocean Grove were business and professional men and their families."[11] Brenda Parnes agrees that "many had above-average incomes."[12] But these statements do not contradict Logan's assertion that those of lesser means found a place at Ocean Grove. One difference between Ocean Grove and other semipermanent meeting grounds was that Ocean Grove was initially conceived as a one-square-mile community that would be filled in an orderly manner with both temporary and permanent structures. This meant the wealthier families could build cottages to which they returned for an extend-

Figure 10. In the early years of Ocean Grove, tents often housed large extended families. Reprinted from Daniels, *The Story of Ocean Grove*, 134.

ed stay every summer, while people of lesser means could stay for a few days in a rented tent.

The survival of a large tent community today is, of course, more than an economic phenomenon. Even the cottages built by those who could afford elegant summer homes maintained the economical use of interior space, exceptionally large openings, minimal lot size, and thin, uninsulated walls of tents. The minimalism of both the tents and cottages of Ocean Grove repre-sented the concept of perfection—in particular, the perfected home life—to day visitors to the campgrounds. The open tent flap or door invited out-siders to gaze at postcard-perfect settings of the family reading, talking, pray-ing, and eating together. Ellen Weiss says of campground architecture:

> Visitors were invited to stare into the cottages as they would into cages at a zoo while the inhabitants returned the stares with stoic in-difference. "Here we are, come look at us! We have nothing to con-ceal!" seemed written over every portal. When a writer suggested that Barnum should hire the little city and show it in Central Park, one understands that he meant complete with inhabitants, an anthropo-logical exhibit.[13]

Likewise, an early guest to Ocean Grove recorded in 1875 that the cottages "all resembl[ed] each other in the folding-doors which stand open most of

Figure 11. The cottage of J. R. Daniels on Pitman Avenue near the ocean is an example of campground cottage architecture in Ocean Grove. Reprinted from Daniels, *The Story of Ocean Grove,* 114.

the time, and show the tastefully-arranged interiors, and the occupants at their various occupations."[14] During services, the families on their tent porches formed dutiful tableaux vivants of the faithful participating in the preaching, singing, and testimony of the camp meeting. For some guests, the architecture itself was a model of perfection. Weiss describes how at night "a wakeful seeker, suffering from awareness of his sins, could find in the glowing tents fresh hope that his struggle to break the chain of a selfish nature would end in victory. The lamps of night still offered a route to redemption."[15] The tents, whether displaying domesticity or devotion, created a perfect picture of the citizens and dwellings of the new Jerusalem-by-the-sea.

Although these holiness seekers sought to embody perfection in domestic and religious architecture, the desire to represent the sacred physically in order to make it present runs counter to Protestant theology. This sacramental view of space and image is evident in liturgical space throughout

Christendom until the time of the Reformation. Protestant reformers, however, rejected the notion that the physical environment conveyed the sacred. It is somewhat suprising then to find significant parallels between Ocean Grove and pre-Reformation attitudes toward the relationship of space to the sacred. One of the clearest statements of this relationship comes at the beginning of the Gothic period when Abbot Suger of St. Denis articulated a theology of architecture in which sacred space and objects could move the faithful from the mundane to the divine.

> Bright is the noble work; but being nobly bright,
> Should brighten the minds, so that they may travel,
>   through the true lights,
> To the True Light where Christ is the true door.[16]

The geometry of space, filtered light, and elaborate statuary of the Gothic style provided intermediary access to God's presence. Calling this theology idolatry, Protestant reformers stripped churches of their images. John Calvin penned perhaps the most succinct argument against the visual; citing the second commandment, he insisted that the spiritual dimension could not be depicted and that any effort to do so was idolatrous.[17] Even Swiss Reformer Huldreich (Ulrich) Zwingli, a professional musician, had the walls of Zurich's cathedral whitewashed and its organ removed. The liturgical space that Reformation Protestants created for themselves was purely utilitarian, devoid of decoration, images, and sculpture. The dominant feature in Protestant architecture from the seventeenth century onward was the pulpit. In fact, the tabernacles and auditoriums of camp-meeting architecture were extensions of the covered preaching platforms enlarged to enormous dimensions.

But however much the reformers whitewashed sacred space and dislocated worship through circuit riders, river baptisms, and camp meetings, they never entirely banished the sacred from American evangelical architecture. Even in the woods, the sacred was visibly represented through the creative shaping of environment—a circle of canvas tents, an elevated wooden preacher's stand, the jumble of produce and whiskey sellers just outside the perimeter, the plank seating that separated males and females, blacks and whites, and the brush arbor "cathedral in the wilderness." Likewise, the landscape of interiors, exteriors, streets, parks, and beaches of Ocean Grove conspicuously displayed a particular image of the sacred. From the ethereal glow of tents to the perfect grid of avenues, the architecture of holiness presented a powerful model of the divine city of God lifted above the disorderly confusion and corrupting influences of the city.

GROUND PLAN OF CAMP GROUND, 131 BY 264 FEET:

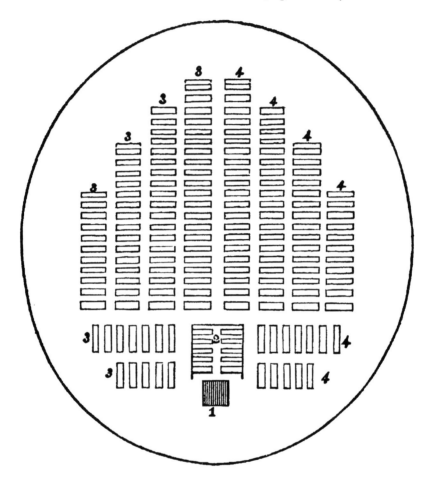

LEGEND:

1. Stand, or speakers' platform.
2. Altar.
3. Seats—ladies' side.
4. Seats—gentlemen's side.
C. Circle on the outside of which the tents are to be built.

Figure 12. Gorham's diagram of a camp meeting. Reprinted from Gorham, *Camp Meeting Manual*, 135.

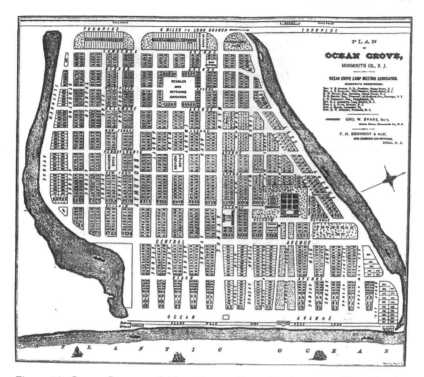

Figure 13. Ocean Grove was laid out in a perfect grid of avenues. The setback increased in the last two blocks to the ocean so that cottage dwellers further inland could enjoy sea breezes and ocean views. The plan also shows the three bodies of water and turnpike that surround the community. Reprinted from *Ocean Grove Annual Report,* 1881, following 62.

The architecture of holiness represented the mythic pilgrimage dwellings of God's people while also displaying a picture of perfect citizens in the perfect city to come. But it was not simply a passive model. The tents, cottages, hotels, roominghouses, auditoriums, and landscape were instrumental in creating specific performances of conversion/holiness. At frontier meetings, tents ringed the campground clearing, forming the threshold of sacred space. This circle of tents contained and focused religious activity like a large parabolic dish, driving the emotional energy back toward the center of the arena. Only by crossing outside this circle of tents could one escape the pressing calls for total involvement in a ritual performance. Outside this boundary were the profane activities that inevitably accompanied camp meetings. Exiting the frontier tent, one immediately entered the arena of the almost continuous flow of revival events. Families withdrew to their tents to rest, but the tents were clearly within the sacred space. Gorham's schedule of activities included meetings of families within the tents. When the tent flap was open, it was possible to remain inside and still see, hear, and participate in the ongoing revival activities. During religious meetings, the tents circling the auditorium offered choice "box seats" for the devout seekers of perfection. Likewise, at Ocean Grove today, the tents form a buffer around the center of religious activity, the auditorium. Tenters still participate in the Sunday morning service while sitting in their tents' living rooms and on their porches, which are extensions of the auditorium's congregational seating. The wide doors of the auditorium allow tenters to take in the pleasant breezes and the holiness preaching at the same time. Only faithful participants in the camp meeting are granted tent leases. Those who moved to Ocean Grove in the 1990s just to enjoy a quiet Victorian community live in apartments or houses outside the tent area.

The architecture at Ocean Grove demanded that tenants make a continual accounting to their neighbors. The walls of one tent were only inches away from the one next to it, and cottages were constructed on small plots at arm's length from neighboring buildings. Although the cottages had solid walls, they had no insulation or interior paneling and thus offered little more soundproofing than the tents. People who chose to live in Ocean Grove were willing to submit to the Methodist discipline of accountability not just at a weekday society meeting but around the clock.

For women especially, tent and cottage architecture was an essential component in the performance of holy leisure at Ocean Grove because it enabled them to live a wholly different existence from the one they knew in the city. Maintaining a two-room tent or a five-room cottage still left them with considerable time for mothers' meetings, family prayers, temperance and suffrage meetings, and seaside recreations. An early guest, writing in 1880, described how "everything is brought to your door . . . and our housekeeping in our little home was without care or fatigue." Early every morning, the muffin man called out, "Hot corn muffins, hot rolls!" And market wagons from local farms made the rounds with fresh fruits and vegetables. Communal meals in boarding tents further reduced a housekeeper's work. Camp-meeting architecture meant that, after a "hasty morning toilet," women were free to chat, take breakfast, walk to the ocean, or attend religious services.[18] After seventy-five years, the author of the *Diamond Jubilee History* of Ocean Grove wrote, "Housekeeping in the tents is simple so that the housewife has freedom for the services and recreation."[19]

As if anticipating that worshipers might gaze at the beams and supports in the auditorium ceiling, the builders of Ocean Grove adorned their

Figure 14. The close proximity of Ocean Grove tents requires accountability to one's neighbors. Photograph by Troy Messenger.

structures with sacred writings. An early account in the *Ocean Grove Record* explained that, eschewing artistic arches, pillars, or scrollwork that "might meet and arrest the wandering gaze, a very happily conceived series of Scripture texts have been painted on the stand, the whole forming a comprehensive gospel, and an evangelical creed for the various denominations which here join in acts of devotion. The motto, 'Holiness to the Lord,' takes precedence."[20] This phrase was associated with the holiness movement from the mid-nineteenth century and was frequently used in connection with the house-based holiness meetings modeled after Phoebe Palmer's Tuesday meetings.[21] In 1880, President Stokes could say that "upon all things connected with us we desire to have written 'Holiness unto the Lord.'"[22]

Apparently, inscriptions were painted on all four auditoriums. On 2 July 1876, for the first service in the second auditorium, Stokes titled his sermon "'All the passages painted on the stand'—there having been stenciled on the rafters various passages of Scripture."[23] A contemporary newspaper account records that the inscriptions included a paraphrase of Hebrews 12:22–24:

> City of the living God
> The heavenly . . .
> The new convenant
> and to the blood of sprinkling.[24]

Likewise, at the Young People's Temple, the rafters on either side of the plat-form bore this inscription:

> Sow a thought, Reap an act.
> Sow an act, Reap a habit.
> Sow a habit, Reap a character.
> Sow a character, Reap a destiny.

In this building, Ocean Grove leaders provided a full program of activities for high school and college youth, who often gathered here six days a week, summer after summer. Even today, many years after this building was de-stroyed by fire, former participants in the youth programs can recite these words.

Weiss records a similar use of text as a scenic element in the annual cottage-illumination festival at Wesleyan Grove. She describes banners on cottages sporting mottoes such as "The Vineyard is our resting place, Heaven is our home" and "We'll camp awhile in the wilderness and then we are going home." At Wesleyan Grove, not all these slogans were religious. Weiss continues, "Messages were a mix of religious sentiment, summer celebra-tion, hometown boosterism, and punster fun."[25]

Text also was used as an interior and exterior decorative element on the cottages of Ocean Grove. For example, in a structure at 58 Heck Avenue, scriptural texts adorn the ceiling beams. At another home, text was embell-ished with floral designs and decorative patterns. The best example of this tradition is found today at 15 Ocean Pathway, one block from the audito-rium; the exterior of this festively painted Victorian boasts elaborate hand-painted flowers and text, and on its steps are these words of Stokes:

> Sun, earth and air, combining with the dew,
> Unfold the seeds, then stem, and bud, and bloom.
> Exquisite tints, pink, violet, and blue,
> Smile in the light, and breathe their rich perfume.
> So, by the sea, in love's divine employ,
> Hearts blossom out, in God's enduring joy.

Even the streets helped model perfection in the architecture of holiness at Ocean Grove. Unlike its predecessors on the frontier, or on Martha's Vineyard, Ocean Grove had streets laid at right angles in a perfect grid. Wesleyan Grove had, for example, developed from the ring design that was so successful on the frontier. As the community grew during the 1850s, a sec-ond ring was placed outside the circle of society tents with smaller radial streets extending back through the family tents. This pattern was repeated so

Figure 15. The hand-painted message on the porch steps of 15 Ocean Pathway is that of Rev. Stokes. Photograph by Troy Messenger.

that neighborhoods formed around open circles. Radial streets funneled people toward the center, while tangential streets allowed flow between the different areas. This innovative pattern was widely imitated in the postbellum years as holiness leaders began residential camp meetings throughout the north. Weiss suggests that the layout was "the direct projection of the usual pattern of action and energy at a revival."[26] Indeed, the pattern facilitated the flow of individuals and actions from tents to a spiritual center, where every action was focused on the conversion experience. Ocean Grove's radically different plan projects the action and energy of a quite different revival—the holiness revival for the perfection of the already converted.

Because conversion and perfection are dissimilar religious experiences, they required different ritual space. Conversion, at least as it was experienced by many participants in early meetings, was a radical philosophical and emotional transformation often accompanied by ecstatic physical manifestations. The path leading from the whiskey seller through the circle of tents to the crowd of listeners to the mourners' bench represented a movement toward both the center of the ritual action and conversion.

Perfection, on the other hand, was the extension of an experience already in process in the life of the holiness seeker. Although many in Phoebe Palmer's Tuesday meetings could cite a specific time when they were perfected, many more could not. Moreover, the perfected did not have to undergo a radical transformation of character; perfection confirmed that they had already become whom they sought to be. The holiness classes and other society meetings where Methodists sought perfection were respectable gatherings of respectable people. The societies used mutual accountability, disciplined study, regular worship, and ordered living to move together toward perfection. In contrast to the conversion model at Wesleyan Grove, this pattern of disciplined, ordered corporate living became the model of ritual experience at Ocean Grove. Here, the preference for a grid of streets and avenues reveals an order and hierarchy that model the holiness experience. The emphasis has moved from a radical individual transformation to a slow modification of communal life. The families of each dwelling are accountable to the next in a highly ordered community where everything is in its place.

Ocean Grove was founded in a period of theological and cultural controversy. The new voices of Darwinian evolution, cultural pluralism, and biblical criticism that arose after midcentury challenged the authority of Scripture and even the primacy of humanity. At Ocean Grove, the evangelical response to these challenges was to retreat to a community where everything resumed its "rightful" place. Mirroring the evangelical world's restatement of its beliefs in increasingly rigid formulas, residents of Ocean Grove could be in no doubt that the perfect city was a city of order—perfectly straight lines intersecting other lines at right angles, defining a series of identical rectangular lots. The meandering, undulating doubts and arguments of the world had no place in the perfect city, where right and wrong were explicit in revivalist rhetoric, and acceptable and nonacceptable behavior were clearly ordained in camp-meeting regulations.

The grid of perfect lines and angles that overlay the natural landscape encouraged some of the largest and most colorful performances in Ocean Grove. These commemorations allowed the community to create moving models of civic hierarchy. For example, on national holidays such as the Fourth of July, Ocean Grove was able to exhibit loyalty both to the nation and to itself.[27] For the centennial Fourth of July celebration in 1876, a parade from Asbury Park to Ocean Grove was led by the marshal and military personnel, followed by Ocean Grove association officers, Asbury Park commissioners, distinguished guests, the goddess of Liberty, thirteen girls representing the original states, the fire departments, day and Sabbath schools, Masons, knights, presses, and, finally, representatives of the trades.[28] Susan Davis has shown the power of parades in performing and negotiating social relations in nineteenth-century America. The recognizable patterns of order in these processions communicated a symbolic understanding of society. Davis states that dividing the line into a sequence of units moving in step implied "unanimity, collective control, and self-control."[29] Thus, the placement of military and Ocean Grove officers at the front and the others following according to organization or trade displayed a publicly acceptable model of Ocean Grove society. Visits by Presidents of the United States and the sea of patriotic banners in the auditorium further demonstrated this alloy of the civic and the religious. Performances such as this were civic advertisements for the new Jerusalem, a theocratic city in a benevolent state where every person had an appropriate place.

Whether in their tents, gathered in worship, or lining the streets, residents saw an image of the divine city while living within it. The utopian community of tent dwellers could not be easily mistaken for the apocalyptic tenements, offices, and streets of New York or Philadelphia. The boundaries of Ocean Grove marked a space modeled on a different vision. The ordering of time and space at Ocean Grove was an intentional adaptation of these elements for a specific end—to create a model of perfection to which residents could aspire. The temporal and physical architecture of Ocean Grove required certain manifestations of holy leisure in the everyday lives of the people who chose to live there. The people who performed acts of perfection within an architecture of holiness did, in fact, become models of perfect people. They were accountable. They marched in perfect order. They read the Bible even while looking at the ceiling or the preacher's stand. They communed with the trees, sand, water, and air of God's Square Mile. The built environment required this perfection, and these actions hallowed the people of the Grove and the place of their meeting.

PART II

PERFORMING HOLINESS

4

BODY AND SOUL

When I can read my title clear to mansions in the skies,
I'll bid farewell to ev'ry fear, and wipe my weeping eyes. . . .

There shall I bathe my weary soul in seas of heav'nly rest,
And not a wave of trouble roll across my peaceful breast.

Isaac Watts, 1707

A striking feature of Ocean Grove is its orientation both by and toward the *sea*. By contrast, at Wesleyan Grove on Martha's Vineyard, the meeting grounds were arranged so that people sat with their backs to the water because the noisy ocean might distract them from the work of the spirit. At Ocean Grove, the water actually became a means of grace. The sea gave new life to the body, just as preaching and prayer gave new life to the spirit. It provided abundant fresh air, healing waters, physical exercise, and opportunities for community interaction. The triumphant Great Auditorium at one end of the wide Ocean Pathway and the clean sand beach at the other marked the two poles of holy leisure at Ocean Grove, where perfected spirits and perfected bodies lived in a community whose order and discipline was modeled not only in worship but also in play.

Camp meetings, from the boisterous Cane Ridge assembly to the embryonic suburbia on Martha's Vineyard, had always been places to "exercise" both body and spirit. But during the first three-quarters of the nineteenth century, between the heyday of Cane Ridge and the establishment of Ocean Grove, attitudes toward the human body changed profoundly. In response to the physical problems caused by the rapid industrialization of the urban east, Christian and secular moralists proposed a host of remedies. At Ocean Grove, the body once again became the domain of the spirit. The sea, in particular, provided a means to restore muscles to Christianity. Yet this reintegration

Figure 16. A souvenir postcard showing the beach and boardwalk in Ocean Grove in the late nineteenth century. Reprinted from Daniels, *The Story of Ocean Grove,* 93.

of the spirit into the living bodies of the holy created performances quite different from the movement of the spirit in backwoods Kentucky.

From Exercises to Exercise

At the earliest meetings, ecstatic movements assured the participants that God was present and transforming. All observers of the first decade of camp meetings include descriptions of the performances of the body during the conversion process. Even more than preaching, singing seemed to stimulate these movements, known collectively as "exercises." Charles Johnson records that during the simultaneous singing of six or more of Watts's hymns, women in their frantic agitations "unconsciously tore open their bosoms and assumed indelicate attitudes."[1] Dickson Bruce Jr. agrees that "the conversions which took place at camp-meetings were highly visible, invariably accompanied by exhibitions of 'acrobatic Christianity,' including jerks, falling, dancing, and barking. Indeed, such displays were taken as signs of conversion."[2] Peter Cartwright, a revivalist preacher whose *Autobiography* chronicled the camp-meeting movement from the beginning of the nineteenth century, commented that, at Cane Ridge in 1801, hundreds fell prostrate at a time as if "men slain in battle."[3]

Those subject to the falling exercise might lie in a trance for anywhere from fifteen minutes to twenty-four hours. There was, in fact, a special group of "exhorters" whose duty was the "recovery" of those convicted sinners whose bodies were held captive by the movement of the spirit.[4] In James Finley's autobiographical account, the first evidence of his impending conversion in 1801 was physical: "While witnessing these scenes, a peculiarly strange sensation, such as I had never felt before, came over me." Embarrassed, he quickly removed himself to a tavern for a bracing shot of whiskey. But the feeling did not subside and eventually he gave in; as soon as his knees hit the ground, he "fell prostrate." An understanding neighbor carried him to a bed where he lay until "suddenly [his] load was gone." A few days later, when he felt the "witness of the Spirit," he "fell [his] whole length in the snow, and shouted and praised God so loud, that [he] was heard over the neighborhood."[5] Throughout these accounts, spiritual conversion had obvious bodily consequences that often *preceded* conscious efforts on the part of the individual to seek the divine. In other words, the body manifested the first signs of an irresistible grace.

In moving to a position of prominence and acceptability in the urban east, the Methodist church eschewed an engagement of the body in spiritual exercises. Achieving respectability in the city meant not only banning the whiskey seller from the perimeter of the camp grounds but also forbidding the disrobing of women in the ecstasy of hymn singing and the spectacle of men on all fours barking the devil up a tree. By midcentury, evidence of conversion and perfection in holiness was claimed by faith, even if no tangible physical sensation accompanied that transformation.

At the same time the body was becoming increasingly separated from the spirit in respectable worship, it was undergoing a similar fragmentation from other spheres of life. The rise of industrial capitalism meant that the body was forced to assume a respectability at work that paralleled the respectability of the pew. Alcohol, once a requisite part of American commerce, was banned from the work place as industrialists led the early temperance movement of the 1830s.[6] Intense physical labor punctuated by brawls gave way to the disciplined performance of repetitive tasks in mechanized environments or hours of sedentary work in enclosed offices. This change was most evident in the northeast, where by 1860 half the population lived in urban areas. Although many argued that "brain work" was superior to physical labor, there were questions about the ill effects of such work on the body.[7] Religion and labor had successfully brought the body under control, yet some considered this subjugation of the body a sign of the physical and moral demise of the American people. The social reformers were united in their belief that the body was more than a container and that its form could be so perfected that people could improve their lives both here and in the beyond.[8]

Roberta Park's history of physical education in America charts the gradual acceptance of the body as part of public and collegiate education through the nineteenth century. She marks the beginning of this movement as 1809, with Joseph Neef's pioneering attempt to integrate physical exercises and games into the teaching of young people. He later joined William Maclure and Robert Owen to found the community at New Harmony, Indiana, in 1826. The years between 1826 and the Civil War saw the establishment of scores of nonreligious utopian communities, most of which also emphasized "pleasant physical exercise and elevating recreations" for both young and old.[9] The success of the physical-education movement in linking exercise and recreation of the body to personal well-being paved the way for a reconsideration of the relationship between bodily and spiritual health.

Perhaps the most outspoken proponent of the relationship between a healthy body and moral virtue was Catharine Beecher, daughter of the well-known minister Lyman Beecher. Writing between 1829 and 1856, she drew unfavorable comparisons between the health of Americans and both their forebears and contemporary Europeans. American children were becoming "feeble, sickly, and ugly." She sought to remedy this situation through detailed instruction in human physiology and the recommendation of appropriate activities to reverse the physical *and* moral decline.[10]

The writings of Beecher and other educators led to the widespread publication of exercise manuals in the 1850s and 1860s. And a concern for the appropriate development of the body became an accepted part of the curriculum in the antebellum years.[11] Soon, urban athletic clubs were attracting like-minded people to combat "the health and moral hazards of the big city."[12]

The publication of Darwin's *Origin of Species* (1859) and his *Descent of Man and Selection in Relation to Sex* (1871) intensified concern over the physical ability of Americans. These works suggested that the human race could either advance or decline depending on its activities. The very things that often accompanied a rise in economic status—specifically, relocation to the city and sedentary work—seemed most likely to produce a race that would not survive natural selection. Some social commentators saw the pale, weak, sickly body of the urban worker as a warning sign that other countries could supplant America through the course of natural selection. In this climate, the muscular body, shaped by rigorous physical activity, became an icon of hope that physical progress would parallel greater moral and intellectual achievements. For Beecher and other reformers, the perfection of the body had profound religious implications as well. In the spirit of nineteenth-century millennialism, perfected people—those with perfect bodies—could lead society toward perfection in a real and literal sense.

"Muscular Christianity" became an increasingly popular response to many to the threats of natural selection, particularly in the north during the second half of the century. The concept had originated in England around 1804 with the fictional hero Tom Brown, who appeared in dozens of books as an ideal male who was both perfectly fit and perfectly moral. In 1857, Charles Kingsley, who coined the term muscular Christianity, wrote the novel *Two Years Ago;* it "revolved about the assumption that morality was a function of muscularity as well as of piety, and that the best sort of Christians were physically fit."[13] Harvey Green quotes a book review in *Godey's Lady's Book* to show that, by 1870, muscular Christianity was "so popular with nearly all classes of people" that books on "bodily strength and skill will find abundant favor."[14]

In contrast to the antebellum emphasis on *individual* redemption and renewal as a catalyst for societal regeneration, muscular Christianity in the postwar years was characterized increasingly by *group* movements toward physical and spiritual perfection.[15] Public playgrounds, health associations, athletic clubs, and college sports provided opportunities to rebuild the body and the community at the same time. Ocean Grove crystallized muscular Christianity's aims by creating a public playground contiguous with a utopian community. The entire square mile was a health association where the population could strive together for renewal.

A Good Dose of Water and Air

In addition to the physical exercises reformers advocated to strengthen and sculpt the perfect body were numerous proposals for curing the sickly and preventing the debilitating effects of modern life. Of the many unhealthy qualities of city life, perhaps none was more frightening than the abundant "bad air," because it could not be seen or felt until it had worked its evil. Beecher wrote in 1856, "It is probable that there is no law of health so universally violated by all classes of persons as the one which demands that every pair of lungs should have fresh air at the rate of a hogshead an hour."[16] Beecher feared that artificially heated air from closed wood stoves acted on the "inmates of a room . . . as a slow poison in undermining the constitution." Confined in crowded rooms with no open windows—at home, at work, and even while traveling—people could not get an adequate supply of fresh air. Even when enjoying the recreations of the city, the close quarters of the theatre, the opera, and the ballroom were equally unhealthy because one could not help but breathe "respired" air. Furthermore, the vapors from decaying refuse in the streets of the industrial city carried disease directly into the body through the lungs.[17] Given the potentially harmful effects of the air at home, at work, and in the streets, it is no wonder that many believed "the best treatment for consumption for those who could afford it was to get out of the city or village."[18]

Mark Cook's *Wilderness Cure* describes a young New York reporter afflicted with persistent fever, poor appetite, and a high pulse rate. The protagonist recovers after spending several months in the mountains; his experience parallels the author's own retreat to the "pure air of the tent."[19] Those intimidated by the trials of living in the wild favored Rev. W. H. H. Murray's popular *Adventures in the Wilderness* (1869), which described a wilderness retreat comfortably close to inns and markets that offered the benefits of the outdoors without the inconveniences.

By midcentury, the pure air and serenity of the "wilderness" were available in the middle of the city. Frederick Law Olmsted designed the first major public park in the United States in 1858. The four-and-one-half-mile-long expanse of Central Park was carefully sculpted to present an ideal natural landscape for those without the time and money to make a wilderness retreat. Olmsted, like other public architects of his time, rejected the boisterous playgrounds popular with the ethnic working classes in favor of a landscape that offered access to a natural environment.[20] The open spaces provided the city dweller with fresh air, invigorating cool breezes, and a temporary respite from the "unhealthy" and "artificial" environments of the tenement and office. That the "nature" New Yorkers beheld was the result of meticulous landscaping and bore little resemblance to the original terrain of mid-Manhattan was irrelevant.

For those with sufficient means to temporarily escape the city, seaside resorts offered the convenience of hotel accommodations, sumptuous fare, and popular amusements along with refreshing sea breezes and an uninterrupted horizon of natural beauty, all easily accessible by public transportation. Coney Island acquired its first hotel in 1829 with the construction of the Coney Island House. Popular with the upper classes before the Civil War, Manhattan Beach in particular sought to provide a wholesome environment for physical and moral improvement in the company of equals.[21] In their efforts to create a therapeutic resort, these leisure communities excluded peddlers, pickpockets, buskers, immigrants, and other undesirables.

After the war, the general acceptance of the seaside's open spaces, clean air, and saltwater as a curative, coupled with the less expensive attractions of Brighton Beach, attracted the working classes as well.[22] Middle-class moralists and employers supported weekend visits by laborers to Coney Island as a healthy alternative to bars, theatres, stuffy tenements, and rough playgrounds. Administrators of so-called fresh-air funds began to send poor children not only to mountain retreats but also on excursions to Coney Island. By the 1880s and the advent of inexpensive rail travel, large numbers of the working class were coming to Coney Island; by 1900, it was attracting about half a million city dwellers every weekend.

The civic planners of Ocean Grove carefully designed the avenues to provide the greatest possible access to sea breezes. The straight avenues allowed these breezes to penetrate deep into the community, whereas a radial plan would have dissipated the breezes in the first block. Furthermore, in the first two blocks away from the ocean, the setbacks were regulated so that the greatest number of houses could benefit from cooling breezes and ocean views. (See figure 12.)

The popularity of Coney Island and other seaside resorts with social reformers was also dependent on what was thought to be the therapeutic power of water. In his excellent summary of the importance of water cures in nineteenth-century American therapeutics, Green notes that contemporary writers strenuously urged the populace to practice frequent bathing.[23] John Wesley himself, in *Primitive Physick* (1747), advocated a discipline of water drinking and bathing to accompany the spiritual disciplines.[24] In the nineteenth century, Edward Hitchcock wrote in the *Journal of Health* that warm baths preserved health and that, contrary to opinion, they did not make people more susceptible to colds or other illness. Hitchcock argued that external water treatments were effective because of the relationship of the skin to the internal organs.

> A very superficial knowledge of the close sympathy between the skin on one side and the stomach and lungs on the other will explain to us how serviceable bathing must be to the latter organs by preserving the former in its proper healthy office—cleansing it of all impurities, keeping it soft and its pores open, so as to allow egress to what, if retained, would cause eruptions on the skin itself, and much internal distress and irregularity of most of the functions of the animal economy.[25]

Catharine Beecher likewise felt there was an intimate connection between the inner and outer membranes, writing in 1856 that cleaning the skin was "one way of securing a healthy stomach."[26] Bemoaning the infrequent bathing of most Americans, she asserted that "probably more than one half the American people never wash *the whole body* from one end of the year to the other; the face, neck, arms, and feet being the only portions enjoying this privilege."[27]

In response to such concerns, hydrotherapy rapidly gained in popularity through the 1840s, and became an organized business in the 1850s. Hydropathic physicians established treatment centers, formed societies, and published journals. The range of diseases these doctors claimed to treat was staggering, and their extravagant boasts and promises eventually led to the demise of the treatment in the 1870s—but not before moralists had made clear the irrefutable connection between cleanliness and health, between bodily and spiritual purity.

Holiness at the Beach

When the founders of Ocean Grove began to look for a site for their permanent camp meeting, they considered only coastal areas. Their intention was to use the sea as a means of grace to restore the perfect body and form the perfect community. For these urban ministers, an undeveloped area of the Jersey coast offered the ideal combination of wilderness and convenience. Readily accessible from both Philadelphia and New York City, Ocean Grove offered enough thick brambles, rolling dunes, and crashing surf to give its visitors the opportunity to briefly experience the "rough life" while communing with the natural elements.

The immediacy of these elements at the seaside prompted comparisons to other wilderness retreats. But it is important to note that before the middle of the nineteenth century, there was no notion of a scenic wilderness where one might retire, even if time and money were available. Dona Brown traces the link between aspiring entrepreneurs and artists as they successfully transformed the forbidding White Mountains into consumable scenery.[28] Previously, few had thought to visit the mountains or the sea for their aesthetic beauty or for the good it might do their bodies. The scenic retreat as a health restorative had to be invented, mass-produced, and sold. Alain Corbin charts the "invention" of the sea as a resort in England and on the continent. Like early mountain retreats, where physicians and scientists offered air and water cures, seaside resorts benefited from their association with "scientific" healing. During the early nineteenth century, "a model of self-care was developing [on the seashore] that succeeded or coincided with that of the rustic retreat."[29] In close communion with nature, the body was hardened, cleansed, and renewed. Indeed, Stokes's description of the founding of Ocean Grove cites reasons similar to those that prompted others in midcentury to seek renewal at mountain retreats—solitude among a small group of like-minded friends and access to the primordial powers of unmediated nature.

Corbin rightly notes that the effort to revive the body through (literal) immersion in the natural elements was an ambiguous experience for many. "On the shores of the ocean, visitors [tried] to allay the anxieties aroused by their loss of vigor and the etiolation, pollution, and immorality typical of urban life. Yet this groping quest for harmony between nature and the body paradoxically [left] no place for hedonism."[30] Evangelicals, shaped by centuries of distrust of leisure and the pleasures of the body, experienced profound new sensations as the cold surf pounded their bodies. At the first seaside camp meeting on Martha's Vineyard, the appropriate indulgence in the pleasures and care of the body had been a constant debate. Dona Brown shows that one of the most formidable obstacles to the successful marketing of Wesleyan Grove was the conflict many nineteenth-century evangelical Christians experienced between their sense of who they were, religiously and socially, and the new secular pleasures they found so intriguing as summer vacationers.[31] But a moral commitment to muscular Christianity, articulated so well by Catharine Beecher, doctors, and educators, allowed the pious to take their leisure as they would beneficial medicine. The formation of utopian Christian retreats provided sanctuaries for holiness advocates where they could pursue bodily perfection in conjunction with complete spiritual sanctification. If they enjoyed themselves and felt good while doing so, it was morally justifiable because of the lofty goal.

At Ocean Grove, the sea was indeed fun, but it was also good medicine and one of the essential means of grace. It was both the physical presence of a powerful God who dwelt in the midst of the holy community and also the "balm of Gilead" that brought "sin-sick" souls back to health and strength. The prominence of the sea in the performance of perfection is evident in the frequency with which it appeared in Ocean Grove hymnody. Consider, for example, these words from the popular hymn "Guide Me, O Thou Great Jehovah":

> Open now the crystal fountain,
> Whence the healing waters flow . . . (*OGCS*, 62)

In evangelical theology, water, both in the baptismal font and flowing from God's heavenly throne, conveyed the sacramental power of God as a healing agent, regenerating the soul. At Ocean Grove, the sacramental power of holy water at the foot of Ocean Pathway played an essential counterpoint to the holiness preaching at the other end of the grassy boulevard.

For early visitors, ocean bathing was still a novelty. People had to be taught what to wear, what to do once they were in the water, how long to stay there, and how to avoid sunburn. "Bathing in the Breakers," a 1876 article in the *Ocean Grove Record*, provided all the essential information a novice ocean bather needed to extract the benefits of hydrotherapy. The article told how to read the flags flown in accordance with the tides to indicate when it was safe to swim, suggested bathing before eating rather than after, recommended sudden immersion of the entire body, stipulated the ideal length of the bath to be approximately three to five minutes, and forbade women from the surf before 6 A.M. because "gentlemen have the only privilege of disporting in natural abandon."[32] A later article promised that a sunburned face is the "the indicator of recuperated vigor and health," and reminded the reader that soreness and irritation were a small price to pay for health.[33]

The detail with which people were instructed in the therapeutic "use" of the beach was not unusual. Corbin observes, "At the seaside holiday, even more than in the humidity of the spas, detailed behavioral patterns were codified as part of the quest for well-being."[34] The ocean was a medicine for the body, and its application had to be carefully regulated to provide maximum benefit. Corbin chronicles in fascinating detail the lengths to which scientists and physicians went to determine the proper prescription of ocean therapy for each ailment.[35] Bathers made their way carefully into the surf via ropes suspended over the water on a series of poles. After immersing themselves for only a few minutes, they were expected to get out of the water and into their clothes to avoid an overapplication of this hydrotherapy.

Other accounts of experiences in the water leave little doubt that residents saw it as a health restorative, though these bathers were clearly enjoying themselves at the same time:

> To many persons the daily dip in the tonic salt water, the stimulus of breasting the big waves, or the delicious relaxation of floating, face up, on the buoyant, upbearing element, furnishes the chief refreshment of a seashore holiday. . . . The surf lubricates the joints like oil; grave men fling out their limbs like colts in pastures; dignified women, from the very inspiration of necessity, sport like girls at recess; aged people tumble among the waves till one would think they were only in their teens.[36]

> The boy or girl, pale with study and confinement, dyspeptic from over stimulation of the mental, at the expense of the physical nature, forget all applications, and let the croqueting, boating, strolling by the sea re-create their powers.[37]

> The sanitary effect of sea bathing, properly used, is well known. There are habitues of Ocean Grove, who first visited it as helpless invalids, through paralytic and spinal diseases, etc., and whose ruddy complexions and stalwart, elastic forms are the highest attestations of the good which may be derived when judgment prevails in the luxury of sea-bathing.[38]

Leaving the city to find one's true self in communion with nature was also a way for Ocean Grove residents to model the perfected self. Coming to a place where they could feel the sand between their toes, toss in the waves,

Figure 17. Temporary booths sprang up along the boardwalk to supply bathers with refreshments and other goods after the South End Pavilion was destroyed by fire in 1915. Reprinted from Daniels, *The Story of Ocean Grove*, 153.

and breathe the fresh ocean air was a way of reclaiming a bit of the Edenic communion with nature that they sought with the coming millennium. Floating in the rolling waves was a performance of holiness. Bathers modeled a unity of bodies and environment, a model of holiness not possible in the confines of the urban landscape. At Ocean Grove, the care, exercise, and pleasure of the body were reintegrated into the fabric of the holy life.

On Jordan's Stormy Banks

The chaotic sea was not always a willing actor in this performance of heavenly order and frequently played mischief with boardwalks, pavilions, and ships. Yet the very unpredictability of the sea's power was testimony to the faithful of the immanence of God in nature. Daniels felt that his account of Ocean Grove was not complete without a chapter on the ocean. His 1919 description of an ocean storm echoes nineteenth-century romantic attitudes toward the natural elements as a curative for body and soul.

> From the days of the Hebrew bards, poets the world over have sung of the variableness of the sea. Its everchanging aspect has made it, through all ages and in all languages, the symbol of mutability, of restlessness, caprice, inconstancy and instability. Nevertheless, it is in this very changefulness that its greatest fascination lies. . . .

Figure 18. An early woodcut titled "Frolicking in the Surf." Reprinted from Gibbons, *History of Ocean Grove,* 73.

> You have seen it, some of you who read. You know the tempest's spell, the breathless joy and tingle of it. How valiantly one struggles down to the shore in the teeth of the mad wind! And how tonic and quickening is the sight of the giant forces in their unrestrained play! The sea plunges and roars, thrashed and fretted to a creamy froth, which is sent scudding in white drifts along the smooth beach or tossed in feathery fluffs far up on the land. The timbers of the pier creak and quiver beneath your daring feet. The breakers leap furiously up against the pavilions, shaking their spray above your head, and you laugh at the risk of a drenching. The frosty wind nips your nose and your fingers; it clutches your garments, now threatening to tear them quite away and again whipping them round and round your trammeled limbs; it blows the swirling wet sand stingingly against your half numbed cheeks. Yet still you laugh, and your heart sings exultantly in tune with the thunderous music that envelops you. There is something solemn and awesome about it too, and you feel your soul expand with a new comprehension of elemental things.[39]

On the beaches of Ocean Grove, the weary urban worker, dissipated by the confining buildings, toxic air, lack of exercise, and incessant demands, could restore the body through contact with the raw elements of nature.

If tent living was a bit too close to those raw elements, Ocean Grove guests could, like Rev. Murray, taste the wilderness without giving up the comforts of home. Here, Daniels reminds less-courageous visitors that, from the safety of cottages and seaside hotels,

> the frailest and most delicate sea-lover can sit all day, warm, sheltered, perfectly protected amid the welter of wind and water in the very wildest weather, and gaze upon the wrack of sea and sky, the wave-torn beach and storm-swept front as far as eye can reach in both directions, without setting foot out of doors, feeling the slightest chill, or drawing in the breath of dampness. And those who saw it thus, as well as we who love to face the blasts, agree that anyone who has never beheld the ocean in a storm has something still to live for.[40]

In addition to Daniels's overwrought accounts were popular music and hymns about the tumultuous sea. One of the most celebrated attractions in Ocean Grove was the annual *Storm* concert by the auditorium organist. When the Hope-Jones organ was installed in the auditorium in 1908, it was the largest pipe organ in the world. The Gibbonses write that "in many respects the Ocean Grove organ is the most wonderful instrument in the world. . . . No organ in the world has the quality of tone colors that this instrument possesses."[41] Indeed, the instrument was, and is, one of the prides of the community and has attracted outstanding organists throughout this century. In addition to its immense size, the organ is also notable for its numerous unusual stops—"ceiling bells, harmonic gongs, drums, singing birds, xylophone, castanets, tambourines, orchestral bells, *surf, thunder and rain effects*"[42] [emphasis mine]—as well as its ability to light the immense American flag mounted on the face of its pipes.

The Storm is a program piece composed by musical director Tali Esen Morgan that enabled audiences to experience the full intensity of ocean weather even on pleasant summer afternoons. It was first performed by Clarence Reynolds in the early 1900s and was played twice daily throughout one week each summer at 4 and 9 P. M. Ticket sales reveal that more than one million people heard performances of the work. The piece, chronicling a day in the life of an army, starts quietly and slowly builds to a dramatic conclusion, with the organist using all the special weather effects. It begins at dawn in an army camp with a bugle sounding reveille and with strains from Grieg's *Morning* and *Peer Gynt*. The organ swells to signal the army on the march. As the army passes through the countryside, church bells chime "America" and "Abide with Me."[43] When the army is once again encamped, the organ leads the company in a celebration of nature and general merrymaking. After the bell sounds five, "Abide with Me" returns, and a funeral march signals that "one of the boys" has gone to his eternal reward. Then the organ begins to unleash the fury of an evening storm. "The rushing wind howls and moans, the rain comes down in torrents, the fearful thunder crashes and vivid lightning flashes combine to make a storm that will not soon be forgotten." After the storm passes, quiet returns with the hymn "Jesus, Savior of My Soul, Let Me to Thy Bosom Fly." The soldier's day ends with the playing of "Taps" and strains of "Home, Sweet Home."[44]

In Christian theology, water has sacramental power to heal, but it also can kill. Even in the healing waters of baptism, water is an ambiguous agent representing both the womb and the grave. At Ocean Grove, God's hand was evident to the faithful both through the life-renewing waves and through the parted seas that led to new life on "the other shore" after death.[45] "Guide Me, O Thou Great Jehovah," for example, not only prays for healing waters but also for God's protection through the storms of life:

> When I tread the verge of Jordan,
>> Bid my anxious fears subside
> Bear me thro' the swelling current
>> Land me safe on Canaan's side. (*OGCS*, 62)

Other hymns use such images as the Flood, the Hebrews' escape through the middle of the sea, Jesus' calming of the waters, and his rescue of Peter out of the stormy waters as metaphors for divine intervention in the midst of threatening forces. Many of the hymns in *Ocean Grove Christian Songs* compare the struggles of the Christian life with the tempestuous sea.

"On Jordan's Banks"

> On Jordan's stormy banks I stand,
>> And cast a wishful eye
> To Canaan's fair and happy land,
>> Where my possessions lie. . . .
> Tho' Jordan's waves around me roll,
>> Fearless I'd launch away. (*OGCS*, 48)

"Home of the Soul"

> I will sing you a song of that beautiful land,
>> The faraway home of the soul,
> Where no storms ever beat on the glittering strand,
>> While the years of eternity roll. (*OGCS*, 53)

"When We Get Home"

> Beyond us lies a fairer shore,
>   Where we will meet when life is o'er.
> There we will rest no more to roam,
>   When we get home.
>
> When there at last we furl our sail,
>   And brave no more the raging gale,
> No stormy sea, no surging foam,
>   When we get home. (*OGCS*, 55)

"Hallelujah to His Name"

> O'er the dashing waters of life's stormy sea,
>   Hallelujah to His Name!
> Still the Master speaketh peace to you and me,
>   Hallelujah to His Name! (*OGCS*, 69)

"Beyond the Tide"

> We are out on the ocean sailing,
>   Homeward bound we sweetly glide;
> We are out on the ocean sailing,
>   To a home beyond the tide.
> We are out on the ocean sailing,
>   To a home beyond the tide.
>
> All the storms will soon be over,
>   Then we'll anchor in the harbor,
> We are out on the ocean sailing,
>   To a home beyond the tide,
> We are out on the ocean sailing,
>   To a home beyond the tide. (*OGCS*, 68)

Indeed, throughout this hymnody is the implicit message that after the storm, "When the Roll Is Called,"

> On that bright and cloudless morning,
>   When the dead in Christ shall rise,
> And the glory of His resurrection share . . . (*OGCS*, 89)

the faithful will stand together with Christ on the "shore" in a land of eternal fair weather. If now we stand "on Jordan's stormy banks," the time will come when we will see the perfect land where "shines one eternal day."

At the first concert recorded in the history of Ocean Grove, the sea played an important role, both literally and figuratively. On a moonless night in the early 1870s, an ambiguous announcement circulated that "nothing particular was to take place" around 10:15 P.M. on the banks of Wesley Lake. As the expectant audience waited, a dozen boats, barely visible in the dark, floated in front of them. A lone voice broke the silence, singing "The Life Boat."

> Again, that persuasive voice repeats "The life boat! the life boat!" Now we think of life's stormy sea and its shipwrecked ones. O from many hearts is wrung the despairing cry, "A life boat!" Is it vain? Does heaven hear? The singer—an unwonted mellowness now in his voice—moves the soul's deep. The lifeboat is near the sinking one. Thank God, he is safe! Join all in the chorus joyfully, for God looks after the shipwrecked.[46]

After a moment of hushed silence, the chorus on the banks joined the voices on the boats in singing,

> Shall we gather at the river,
>   Where bright angel feet have trod;
> With its crystal tide for ever
>   Flowing by the throne of God?
>
> Yes, we'll gather at the river,
>   The beautiful, the beautiful river,
> Gather with the saints at the river
>   that flows by the throne of God. (*VOP*, 1048)

On that note, the concert was over.

Following this first concert, water continued to be the focus of the largest performances at Ocean Grove, among the most popular of which were the grand illuminations of the annual Lake Carnival; these began in the first decades of the community and continued through the early twentieth century. On Martha's Vineyard, an equally popular land-based Illumination began in 1870 with 100 lanterns along Clinton Avenue; by 1874, this had mushroomed into a festival with 3,200 lanterns, fireworks, music, and parades.[47] Ocean Grove visitors familiar with the Wesleyan Grove celebration may well have initiated the Lake Carnival. The Illumination on Martha's Vineyard was characterized by spectators and performers winding their way through the streets of the community to look at stationary lanterns. The Lake Carnival was a water pageant with a stationary audience and a parade of boats. Both events appear to have attracted most of the summer residents along with a large number of guests. The 1877 Illumination drew some thirty thousand additional guests to Martha's Vineyard for the one-day event, a crowd so large that many visitors had no place to spend the night.[48] The *Ocean Grove Record* reported that forty thousand people lined the banks of Wesley Lake for the Carnival of 1885. (The religious services of camp-meeting week in the last quarter of the nineteenth century also attracted huge crowds, but almost never more than ten to twelve thousand.) Every house and hotel was decorated. Fireworks exploded overhead, and bands played from the decks of the 300 boats illuminated by Chinese lanterns.[49] In 1903, electric fountains were placed in the lake at each end of the parade.[50] The following year, three decades after the first concert on Wesley Lake, the boat carnival still drew between twenty and thirty thousand.[51]

No doubt, the thousands of lanterns, immense crowds, fireworks, and pageantry had a tremendous impact on the late-nineteenth-century spectator. Yet Ellen Weiss maintains that the crowds took all this in with "strict decorum and quietness"; the majestic illuminations were greeted with "dazed silence, the sense of utter amazement, the unreality of this exotic place. It was an upgraded and opulent version of the 'phantasmagoria of light and beauty' of the lighted tents of the 1850s and of the nighttime theater of the first camp meetings."[52]

These evening illuminations took place the week before the beginning of the camp-meeting revival, bringing to a climax the period of "rustification" and relaxation and marking the shift in emphasis from perfection of body to perfection of spirit. In these pivotal performances, as in the physical layout of the communities, Ocean Grove differed from Wesleyan Grove in its orientation toward water. In Ocean Grove, the transformation of the water environment with floating and exploding lights made visible the transformative power of water on individuals who had spent their summer months bathing in its healing streams. The silence of the observers of such a spectacular display signals a particular understanding of and participation in these events. The spectators were themselves part of the performance, and their silence and self-imposed order model a view of perfection that equates decorum with the holy. The gathered thousands modeled a particular version of the citizens of the heavenly city by quietly absorbing the emotional impact of the event without exhibiting any external physical sign. In fact, this behavior exactly duplicated the congregational response to the display of God's presence in Ocean Grove's camp-meeting revival services. For example, in 1894, at the first service in the newly opened auditorium, seven to eight thousand people worshiped "without the sound of a foot-fall or confusion of any kind. The Lord is in His holy temple."[53] If the Carnival marked the end of the leisure half of the summer and the beginning of the holy week, it also demonstrated that the two were inextricably linked. Carnival displayed the sacramental power of water leisure and the people responded with reverence, just as they did to the evidence of God's spirit in hymn singing or preaching.

At the beginning of the nineteenth century, it was believed that an individual's inability to control the spirit's action on and through his or her body was a testimony to the renewing graces of God. Thirty years later, the body was divorced from the work of the spirit. But by the last quarter of the century, the body was once again the terrain of God's spirit, and the spirit-filled body responded to the irresistible graces of the spirit's activity. Now, however, the model was completely different: the holy body was quiet, orderly, at peace, restored to health because the action of the spirit on the body subdued any violent impulses to lawlessness or sin. To reach this state of bodily perfection, holy water had to replace the stresses and evil influences of the urban environment.

With the beginning of camp-meeting week, Carnival lanterns were extinguished, and summer guests turned their attention to the plethora of religious meetings, from private devotions upon waking to twilight meetings before retiring. The legacy of Gorham's schedule for camp-meeting worship is still evident today in the many religious offerings throughout the days of camp meeting. But the sea was not abandoned for the sake of worship; nor was the body abandoned for the spirit. On Sunday evenings around six, the community gathered at the shore for surf meeting, a relatively informal service consisting of hymn singing, testimonies, prayer, and preaching. Daniels describes the meetings as a "social gathering as well as a religious service" that might be interrupted by the blast from an ocean steamer responding to the handkerchief salute on shore or the laughter that arose when an "unusually audacious wave" would drench those nearest the water's edge.[54] Early photographs show attendees talking among themselves, walking along the sand, and facing the ocean, even when that meant turning away from the preacher's stand. With five thousand people present and the surf "rolling up and dashing on the beach with measured tone," it must have been difficult if not impossible to hear the preacher. Only as the group joined in singing could the assembled have turned their attention from the sea to the spirit. But even then,

> Beside the sea the wondering people stood,
>> Or sat, or bowed, devotion's earnest throng;
> The spirit, lost in worship's attitude,
>> Mingled its praises with the billows' song.[55]

Figure 19. The surf meeting in 1878. Reprinted from Daniels, *The Story of Ocean Grove,* 83.

By all accounts, the sea was (and is) one of the foremost attractions of Ocean Grove. Nineteenth-century visitors to the Grove used it to attempt to create the perfect body—healthy, strong, and at home in its environment. For the pious Ocean Grover, the sea revealed the powerful presence of God, both as hydropathic healer and as omnipotent sovereign. The seaside retreat was part of a larger system that included movements in calisthenics, diet, gymnastics, athletics, and medicine. The aim of this muscular Christianity was to build perfect citizens for the coming kingdom. These citizens modeled perfection by coming to the beach—to play, to enjoy spectacles, and to worship; to them, the activity was a means of grace that perfected body and soul. Holy leisure by the sea was part of a systematic effort to build holy men, who could guard the gates of holiness against the powers of evil, and holy women, who could bear the children of righteousness.

5

MALE AND FEMALE

Men and women who were housed in the same architecture of holiness, who worshiped and played together, bathed at the same beaches, and marched on the same streets might be expected to reach perfection in much the same way at Ocean Grove. And once attained, that perfection would presumably be consistent, regardless of gender. To some degree, this was so. Boys and girls alike refrained from Sunday card playing and beach going. Both women and men prayed, sang, and heard holiness preaching in an environment of mutual support and accountability. Yet in many other instances, the performances of holy leisure reveal quite different manifestations of perfection with respect to gender. Given the dichotomy between women and men in most other areas of nineteenth-century life, perhaps it is not surprising that, even in a perfected community, traditional gender roles would pertain.

At Ocean Grove, there were male and female ways of participating in worship, male and female possibilities for community pageantry, male and female forms of tent life, male and female ways of going to the beach, and male and female reform movements. But these gendered performances of holy leisure were not a simple mirroring of heterosexual nineteenth-century American culture. Rather, the gendered expression of popular piety was yet another way the people at Ocean Grove distinguished themselves from secular society and modeled a perfected home life where each gender had its proper place. The persistence today of many of these gender-specific modes of perfection demonstrates the depth of gender presuppositions in the culture of holy leisure and the importance of gender models in maintaining this mode of "perfection."

Ocean Grove's earliest history articulates a gender typology that consistently appears in the performance of holy leisure. The story of the community's selection and consecration is a foundational myth that incorporates these gendered expressions of piety. The men, including the Reverends Osborn and Stokes, "discovered" the secluded wilderness site and had a vision about establishing a camp meeting here. When the first families arrived at the shore, they set up tents and went several days without any corporate religious meeting. On 31 July 1869, part of the group was on its way down to the sea to enjoy the moonrise when Mrs. Thornley proposed they hold a prayer meeting instead and made a place within her tent for it. Because this account of the "discovery" and consecration of the site functions similarly to a creation story in the social mythology of Ocean Grove, the male and female participants become archetypal characters in the play of gender roles. Within this economy of power, the men are planning and building the environment, but when they go off to enjoy the scenery, the faithful wife calls them to pray. Male and female then gather together within the sanctity of the home.

The gender archetypes in this account reflect attitudes toward gender and religion that developed during nineteenth-century camp meetings. Camp meetings evolved on the frontier in a period when the distinctions between the "immorality" of male life outside the home and the "sanctity" of female domesticity were profound. Johnson describes the frontier as a place of "moral laxity" where "monotonous existence, ceaseless hard labor, and limited sources of amusement also help explain the low moral tone."[1] The popular male recreations of drinking, fighting, and carousing were considered by contemporary women and preachers to typify a "life of sin."[2] Male drinking was particularly pervasive and often excessive. The omnipresent whiskey at log rollings, house raisings, militia musters, cornhuskings, weddings, and funerals often provoked fighting.[3] Dickson Bruce Jr. records that fighting was such a serious problem on the frontier that in one North Carolina county "all but three of sixty-nine indictments were for assault and battery."[4] Bruce further maintains that the hard life noted by Johnson was not the only cause for male drinking and aggression. The violent behavior was an attempt to demonstrate independence in the face of the encroaching demands of nineteenth-century American life. Despite its association with "honor," the male presentation of self outside the home increasingly diverged from the norms of evangelical religion. Except for hunting, all forms of male recreation were condemned from the pulpit as immoral.[5]

Evangelicals strove to bring male recreation closer to the temperament of female recreations, which were centered around home and religion.[6] After all, "the home was a sacred place," and heaven was home lifted to a higher reality—"There's a better home, a'waitin', in the sky, Lord, in the sky."[7] If the sites of male leisure—the field, the town, the tavern—were rife with temptation and sin, the home was a sanctuary of holiness guarded by a vigilant woman. Ted Ownby, in particular, has documented the significance of changing patterns of recreation and piety on the relationship between the sexes. He notes, "Women began to orient themselves to a changing world by rejecting most activities outside the home as threatening and sinful and by celebrating activities within the home."[8] Whether this retreat was from a "heartless" industrial culture in the north or what Ownby calls the "hot-blooded world of male sinfulness" in the south, nineteenth-century holiness was predicated on the notion that women protected and sustained a home-centered morality against the corrupting influences of worldly male sinfulness.

Conversion for men in the camp-meeting theology of the frontier was salvation from this "worldly" life of male vice to a restored relationship "at home" with God and family. Bruce uses a rite-of-passage model to illustrate the conversion formula manifested in early camp meetings.[9] A "life of sin," an essential precondition to this process, was pitted against a strong religious influence, usually a mother or other female figure. In the spiritual autobiographies of the early nineteenth century, these two extremes were gendered. *Boys* experienced the world with little interference from their fathers, but they were the objects of constant prayer from their *mothers*.[10] Out of this tension arose a "conviction" of the world's sinfulness and a desire to separate from one's previous life. This separation created an ambiguity in which the convicted sinner's previous life was negated but a new order was yet to be established. It was in this ambiguous state that the convicted experienced violent spiritual exercises. It was also during this period that the social structure of frontier society was inverted; women had equal authority as preachers as they worked together at camp meetings to exhort and pray convicted sinners to the state of "assurance." Once a person received assurance, he or she was reordered within the new evangelical home-centered social structure.

Every feature of the frontier camp meeting was calculated to facilitate an individual's movement through the conversion process. Since conversion challenged deeply help convictions of maleness in frontier culture, it is somewhat surprising that men were attracted to camp meetings. W. J. Cash, writing in the 1940s about the temperament of the white Southern male, has argued that men who loved "the thrill of the drunken brawl, the cockfight, and the all-night hunt also loved the excitement of the revival meeting."[11]

Indeed, all these pleasures and more appear to have been available outside the protective perimeter of family tents. Yet Ownby correctly counters that male culture was fundamentally at odds with the "home-centered evangelicalism" that religious leaders sought to establish through the camp-meeting experience. In the conversion process, male self-sufficiency and toughness had to be broken. It was also a process of role reversal, in which a man's former life became meaningless. In recognizing this, some men even fell to the ground and sobbed like babies, while women labored tirelessly in prayer and exhortation.

Bruce compares these camp-meeting conversion experiences to other rites of passage; during all such rituals, the social order is temporarily suspended as individuals move from one status to another. While converts are being transformed from sinner to saved, they are neither in their previous state nor the state they will ultimately attain. Their temporary existence in this ambiguous alternative social structure is determined by the ritual action itself. Because initiates have been released from the expectations of their former life but have not yet assumed new responsibilities, this middle ground offers the possibility of experimenting with alternatives to the status quo. Bruce remarks, "The negation of structure in the conversion period must have had the effect of invalidating the secular images of self and society which most plain-folk had. Both men and women were undoubtedly affected by the reversal which found a normally subordinated sex assertive to the point of assuming practical leadership."[12]

Barbara Epstein makes a similar point when she stresses the significance of women's conversion experiences as a challenge to an inherited Puritan/Calvinist social order based on obedience to superiors. Unlike the shared experience of men and women in the eighteenth-century religious awakening, the experience of camp-meeting conversion differed sharply for men and women in the first half of the nineteenth century. Epstein reminds us that in Reformed theology, women were under the headship of their husbands in a hierarchical society in which children submitted to parents, lay to clergy, and ministers to God.[13] This deeply rooted Calvinist theology of mutual dependence meant that everyone assumed her or his place in an unequal division of responsibility and authority. The shift of the New England middle class away from a home-based economy to a society where goods were increasingly produced out of the home meant that a woman's place in society was further circumscribed. While men traveled further afield to pursue business interests, women were encouraged to abandon personal ambition and limit themselves to marriage and motherhood.[14] According to Epstein, "Where for the Puritans, and for the authors of late-eighteenth-century ladies' books, motherhood had been only one of a woman's tasks, nineteenth-century writers saw motherhood as the most important of a woman's responsibilities."[15] Through religious conversion, women played out a cycle of rebellion and submission to this male-dominated social and religious structure. It granted them the authority to speak in areas where they ordinarily could not. And it offered them the power to pray over "lost" husbands and sons. But religion also required them to live in submission to the male heads of families and churches. This struggle between a religiously sanctioned domesticity and an alternative position as the superior religious authority figured in many of the published stories of women's conversions.[16]

After conversion, men were refocused on their responsibilities toward the home while maintaining their position as head of the family. Women, on the other hand, while submitting to male authority within the home, never completely surrendered the authority they had been granted within the camp meeting. After midcentury, women in the holiness movement resumed the freedom they had exercised at the mourners' bench to take the lead in calling the converted from complacency to a place of spiritual perfection. Melvin Dieter recognizes the significance of holiness theology in challenging the authority of the male leadership. He says, "It was the theology of the movement and the essential nature of the place of public testimony in the holiness experience which gave many an otherwise timid woman the authority and the power to speak out 'as the Holy Spirit led her.'"[17] Phoebe Palmer modeled the newly assertive power of women as advocates of holiness with her Tuesday meetings. She wrote a widely read book that claimed the rights of public testimony for women and encouraged Catherine Booth, wife of the leader of the Salvation Army, to begin her public preaching ministry. At her weekly meetings, Palmer used her home as a sacred space for exhorting fellow Christians on to greater holiness. The evolution of home-centered evangelicalism not only challenged male immorality but it also posed a threat to male authority in the pulpit. Palmer successfully refuted male clergy who disliked her parachurch movement, and the Methodist church as a whole eventually accepted her understanding of holiness. As a result of women's effectiveness in holiness work, the holiness churches were among the first to grant women ministerial rights: in the mid-1880s, the Mennonite Brethren in Christ accepted women ministers, and the Nazarene Church followed before the turn of the century.

At Ocean Grove, women's new liberty within the holiness movement was moderated by the Methodist desire for respectability within a wider male-dominated American society. These contradictory trends often existed simultaneously in tension with one another in this community. On one hand, permanent camp meetings sought to institutionalize the glory pen—to provide a space where people could live for months at a time, exhorted by women, preachers, friends, and the environment itself in a utopian community that inverted the norms of urban life.[18] On the other hand, Ocean Grove also wanted to model the home-centered *communitas* that was the end result of camp meetings. After all, the holiness people had already been converted. If this form of evangelicalism used the spiritual strength of women to refocus male morality toward the home, it still created separate and unequal domains within that home for male and female.

A revealing notice in the *Ocean Grove Times* of 8 June 1912 indicated that, due to a shortage of men, the choir would be composed only of women that season.[19] Some long-time residents recall men who continued to commute to the city for work after their families had taken summer residence at the Grove. These men joined their wives and children on the weekend and for shorter stays during their own vacation time. This suggests that Ocean Grove was, to some degree, a community governed and visited by men but inhabited more by women and children.

In his article "The Housing of Gender," Mark Wigley maintains that, from the Renaissance forward, the house has been a place for securing women from the world. Male mobility in the world beyond the home was juxtaposed with female stasis in the interior. Wigley writes that "the house is literally understood as a mechanism for the domestication of (delicately minded and pathologically embodied) women."[20] At first glance, Ocean Grove seems to be something very different. Camp-meeting dwellings were designed to expose occupants to the continual scrutiny of neighbors and day guests. The open doors and tent flaps led immediately into the sleeping quarters and blurred the lines between exterior and interior space. The everyday life of women within this architecture is an undisguised display of domesticity, family piety, submission to the strict rules of community life. At night, tent residents were still visible in the glow of lamplight, even when the tent flaps were closed. At Wesleyan Grove, this infringement on privacy was enforced by an ordinance that required tent residents to keep a light burning throughout the night.[21] Men, on the other hand, lived both inside and outside the camp meeting, sometimes subject to Ocean Grove's rules and sometimes not.

If some men crossed the community's boundaries more often than women did, it still remained their exclusive responsibility to guard the boundaries of space and behavior for those within. Ocean Grove was governed by twenty-six men—thirteen clergymen and thirteen laymen—who constituted the local Camp Meeting Association. Likewise, the police who

Figure 20. President Roosevelt addressing the convention of the National Educational Association in the Great Auditorium, July 7, 1905. Reprinted from Daniels, *The Story of Ocean Grove*, 217.

enforced the rules and guarded the boundaries were male. A tension existed between the interior and exterior because all of Ocean Grove was essentially closed to outsiders but open to those within. The architecture of holiness thus maintained protective walls while simultaneously requiring the mutual accountability of a parlor meeting.

Guarding the community was not the exclusive responsibility of men. Boys were trained from the age of eight as part of Tali Esen Morgan's Rough Riders. Morgan, director of the thousand-member Children's Festival Chorus, found the 300 boys in this group impossible to control, even with four policemen on hand for rehearsals. His solution was to outfit them in khakis and divide them into three troops under the direction of "experienced drill-masters." The group was named the Young Rough Riders in honor of Theodore Roosevelt's company. Daniels says that the move was a great success. "Cops" were no longer needed to police the boys, who were eager to show discipline and character suggestive of Teddy Roosevelt's elite group.[22]

It is telling that Morgan chose Roosevelt's example to channel the aggressive energies of these young boys. A product of Harvard's athletics program, Roosevelt maintained his collegiate enthusiasm for sports and physical training during his political career, when he ardently advocated the "strenuous life" as a curative for the "neurasthenic and dyspeptic American

Figure 21. Some of Ocean Grove's Rough Riders parading down Ocean Pathway. Reprinted from Daniels, *The Story of Ocean Grove*, 165.

male."[23] He led the crusade for a male conquest of the wilderness, believing it would both toughen sedentary urban men and serve as a "safety valve" for their pent-up energies.[24] Characterized by "outings" into undeveloped parts of America or game-hunting expeditions on other continents, his wilderness expeditions sought to mold the character and bodies of young men. As governor of New York State, U.S. president, and colonel of the Rough Riders, Roosevelt epitomized the ideal of muscular Christianity—someone who overcame physical limitations through focused athleticism and engagement with the wilderness to become a skilled leader and protector of the nation. Indeed, Roosevelt's visits to Ocean Grove in 1899 and 1905 are heralded as two of the greatest days in the community's history.[25]

In this male version of muscular Christianity, the energies of young boys had to be directed to productive ends lest the youths turn to crime or immorality. Hardened by the wilderness and disciplined within a military-style hierarchy, they could protect the female-centered home from sin and lawlessness. Uminowicz describes Ocean Grove as "a fortress where Christian soldiers rested, recreated, trained, and were inspired before invading the 'territories of sin.'"[26] Indeed, participation in the Young Rough Riders was training not only for spiritual battles but also for the worldly battles against any threats to the sanctity of the American home. A boy innocently playing soldier on the beach actually represented an important performance of gender identity within the perfectionism of Ocean Grove. Writing immediately after the First World War, Daniels reminds his readers

Figure 22. A boy and girl on Ocean Grove Beach. Reprinted from Daniels, *The Story of Ocean Grove*, 234.

that the distance was not great between this boy and "our boys" on the front lines:

> "Where did you receive your military training?" asked the commanding officer.
>
> "I was a member of Mr. Morgan's Rough Rider military companies at Ocean Grove every summer since I was eight years old," replied the soldier boy.
>
> He was a top sergeant at Camp Wadsworth, Spartanburg, South Carolina. Probably scores—maybe hundreds—of the boys who have been trained in the military companies are now in the service of Uncle Sam. . . .
>
> Little did anyone dream that this training would prepare the boys for this great world's war. It is very certain that few, if any, of these boys were rejected as being unfit for the service, for not only were they trained in military affairs, but they were surrounded by the moral atmosphere and religious character of Ocean Grove.[27]

After boys graduated from the Children's Chorus and the Young Rough Riders, they could (and still can) continue to exercise their military-style maneuvers in another performing ensemble. The Auditorium Ushers are an elite group of Ocean Grove men whose name belies their importance in the structure of Grove society. Daniels describes them in 1919 as "business men" who were "unusually intelligent and capable."[28] These men supplemented the work of the male police force by controlling entry and egress from all worship services and public events in the community. To this day, everyone who enters the auditorium or tabernacle encounters these uniformed men, who always voice a greeting, hand out a program, and offer assistance if needed.

Daniels credits them with an unsurpassed ability to handle the crowds that attended some of the special events in Ocean Grove. Although some promoters wanted to hire their own ushers, the camp meeting encouraged the use of its own men, promising that their "intimate knowledge" of the space and "efficient manner" could not be surpassed.[29] It is fitting that in the Gibbonses' book the ushers are pictured opposite the police, for the two groups of uniformed men perform similar roles for Ocean Grove. Both control the perimeters of Ocean Grove society and mediate access to the holy.

Nowhere in Ocean Grove is the order and authority of male control of boundaries more explicit than in the carefully choreographed movements of the offertory march by the Auditorium Ushers.

> This work has been so thoroughly organized for years that it moves with perfect ease and quietness. As if by magic, the ushers appear at their designated places, the collection is received rapidly and without confusion, after which the ushers gather from all parts of the building at the head of the main aisle, from which place they proceed in orderly fashion to their places before the chancel for the presentation of the offering.[30]

This description in 1919 of what "had always" or "for many years" been an impressive display characterizes the march as it continues to be performed. The wide barnlike doors of the auditorium open every few feet to let in the natural air conditioning from the ocean. At each entrance is one or more attending ushers; likewise, the gallery floor has one or more ushers at the entrance from each staircase. The offering is collected at each worship service in the auditorium. These occasions are typically "preaching" services, with the offertory coming about a third of the way into the service, immediately after a camp-meeting representative gives an official welcome from the pulpit. During the welcome, ushers seat latecomers and then assume their positions at the interior end of each aisle. When the organ begins the offertory music, the hundred or so ushers step into place and move quickly through crowds that number five or six thousand; in the early years, this number sometimes approached twelve thousand. After passing the collection baskets through each row, the ushers pause at the exterior ends of the aisles until all their company is ready. When all the baskets have completed their routes, the men begin filing toward the center of the auditorium, those closer to the

center waiting for those farthest away. As they pass each aisle, men are added
to the line. Each line converges at the center of the auditorium, where it
awaits the completion of the organist's offertory. Then the organ shifts to the
official music for the Ushers' March, which is an odd mixture of Souza and
the fairground.[31] Composed by auditorium organist Clarence Kohlmann in
1941, this piece is performed without fail for every march. After four bars of
fanfare introduction, the head usher raises his right arm across his chest to
signal the second scene in this two-part procession. The twin columns file
down to the front of the auditorium, where the baskets are collected and
then taken out. After all the baskets are gone, the remaining ushers then re-
circle the auditorium, resuming their posts at every portal. The whole performance is carefully timed to be completed before the music ends.

The *Diamond Jubilee History* concludes, "As they stand before the chan-
cel, they give a picture of as fine a group of upstanding men as one could
see."[32] The piece is a marvel of efficiency and order, a perfect model of
Ocean Grove society. The fact that this performance has survived from the
Victorian era virtually unchanged indicates its importance in the community's modeling of perfection for itself. Like other models in Ocean Grove society, the Ushers' March, which continues to be performed, both displays
and creates orders of perfection. In contrast to the unruly frontier gatherings, the ushers' efficient control of the crowds and their ordered movement
through them models a mature, respectable Methodism. The refined civi-
lization of the perfect community is guaranteed by the vigilance of a hundred ushers and is modeled by their steps. Further, by ritually circumscrib-
ing the perimeter of the auditorium, the ushers mark in worship the role
men play throughout Ocean Grove society as guardians of the sacred arena.
They stand at the threshold, just as the police used to do, between public
and sacred precincts.

Beginning in 1899, the community sponsored an annual banquet hon-
oring the ushers and their wives in the week preceding the opening of camp
meeting, when the ushers' responsibilities would be most demanding. One
of the most anticipated features of the banquet was a variety show staged by
the ushers.[33] In the years after the disappearance of the Lake Carnival, the
Ushers' Banquet and Show was a festive means of marking the end of the
recreational pre-meeting period. Beginning in 1943, the ushers' performance
was separated from the banquet and presented in the auditorium to the
entire community, typically on the Saturday eight days before camp meeting; the banquet took place the following Wednesday. The show became
immensely popular and by the mid-1960s attracted four to five thousand
viewers. Show planning usually began with an après-show meeting in

August or September for the following year. Themes were discussed, and costumes, makeup, and scenery were assigned to various subcommittees. By the time most ushers reported for duty on the second Sunday of June, much of the show was already in place. Typically, it began with an opening march and then continued with an array of variety acts including seasonal hits; popular, religious, and stage songs; Rockette-style dance numbers; circus acts; and parodies of other Ocean Grove events.

These performances gave the ushers a chance to play at what they were not, to abandon their quiet, "respectful" poses. One usher remembers fondly that "people loved it. They were the people they knew cavorting around and up the aisle." Even the solemn auditorium march was jazzed up to lyrics by Ted Widland or the lively strains of "When the Saints Go Marching In." The *Ocean Grove Times* reported, "Public response to the staid Sunday ushers in silly Saturday action has always been enthusiastic."[34] The most popular acts featured cross-dressed men in scenes such as the "Womanless Wedding." In 1966, all 100 ushers, including the president, were dressed as girls or women in a show titled "Girls, Girls, Girls" and advertised as portraying the many ages of women. The twenty-fifth anniversary show of 1967 was set at international ports of call with "lads and lassies, or senors and senoritas, or moo-moo girls and beach boys."[35] Other popular features of the Ushers' Shows were the fashion show, bathing beauties, and the Ocean Grove Rockettes. The 1969 version included a parody of the most popular women's processional performance of the summer—the Asbury Park Baby Parade. The last Ushers' Show was held in 1971, and by 1974, the Camp Meeting Association had supplanted homespun vaudeville with professional rock concerts.[36]

The sight of otherwise serious men in coconut bras, baby bonnets, and evening gowns singing and dancing to popular show tunes must certainly have been a humorous highlight of the summer season. The inversion of these shows—the caricaturing of women by the male ushers—underscores important attitudes toward gender in the model of perfection. The comic skits about moo-moo girls, Rockettes, fashion models, and brides reflected an image of women as entertaining, happy, and at home. But what never appeared on the stage of the Ushers' Show were the issues of social advocacy that women began to exercise in a Victorian age of protofeminism. The performers did not play Phoebe Palmer, women preachers, suffragettes, or temperance workers. Even in satire, the Ushers' Show continued to model women within the evangelical structure of domesticity. Moreover, although men had an opportunity to perform female stereotypes, women's performances did not permit them to model or explicitly challenge the roles of their men.

Although the inversion offered a glimpse at an alternative reality where men were willing to assume the "feminine" roles of entertainer, bride, and mother, it nevertheless reinforced the men's authority as official interpreters of the vision of community.

Women too had an opportunity to create community performances. The largest of these was the annual Baby Parade along the boardwalk from Asbury Park to Ocean Grove. In 1890, Asbury Park founder James Bradley led a procession of 200 infants in the first annual Baby Parade. Infants dressed as various flowers and fruits rode in carriages festooned with "flowers, flags, and bunting."[37] The parade grew quickly and by 1912 included 700 infants and boasted 150,000 spectators.

In the early years of the twentieth century, the two communities continued to cooperate for this event and began to incorporate other festivities around it. The 1903 celebration, for example, included a Wednesday evening reception for the Carnival Queen, a Thursday afternoon parade of fire equipment, and a Thursday evening masked fête at each of the big hotels in Asbury.[38] In 1904, the Baby Parade was part of a Mardi Gras week, which included numerous children's events and shared front-page headlines of the *Ocean Grove Times* with a report on the close of camp-meeting week.[39] In the following years, several of these events became staples of the week-long festival—most notably, the Carnival on the Asbury boardwalk, the Baby Parade, and a culminating pageant in the Ocean Grove auditorium for the coronation of Titania, queen of the fairies. The 1906 activities included the Children's Festival Chorus of one thousand members, "a 'chorus of Maidens' in Indian costume, the 'Mandoline Club of young ladies,' and the Boys' Rough Riders Company."[40] By 1912, there were two Carnival coronations, apparently at the beginning and end of the week's festival. The *Ocean Grove Times* described the first of these performances, the "Crowning of Titania":

> Carnival Queen entertained with a program in which surprise followed surprise—Geisha Girls, Indian Squaws and Braves, Spanish senoritas, Gypsy Maidens, Colonial Squires and Dames, make their initial bow to royalty—handsome decorations, splendid electrical effects, and a riot of life, light and color.[41]

This performance attracted eleven thousand people, and a week later, the "Fairyland Festival," also featuring the crowning of a fairy queen, was attended by eight thousand.[42]

The parade and children's pageants underscored the reputation of the two communities as *family* resorts. Moreover, it was a community model of the perfected family. The proliferation of babies suggested that the seaside stay had restored women to their natural place as "fit mothers." Unbound from corsets, energized by healthful exercise, and purified by clean ocean air, the female half of muscular Christianity was ready to give birth—abundantly.

Bearing children, parading them in the streets, and organizing huge pageants for adolescents was a way for women to model Victorian attitudes toward domesticity and child-rearing. As Christine Stansell has shown, the streets of nineteenth-century New York were an arena of opposing attitudes toward children.[43] The children who roamed city streets—playing, huckstering, and sometimes stealing or worse—were evidence to middle-class evangelicals of moral failure on the part of their working-class parents. To these moralists, the home was a sacred domain that guarded children from the ills of society.[44] Children whose mothers worked often had to work themselves, and did not receive the home-based nurture that social reformers insisted was necessary to their moral and spiritual development. In New York City, the triumph of these reformers in securing public space signaled both the dominance of the middle class and of a conception of women as nurturing mothers within the home.[45] In Ocean Grove, pious Christian reformers also used the streets to model the same ideals of gender and domesticity. Uminowicz agrees that the "'great warm wave of infancy' served as a metaphor for the successful 'cultivation' of children."[46] As a setting for the Baby Parade and children's pageants, the streets of Ocean Grove displayed perfect homes where fit women bore healthy children, nurtured them, and engaged them in uplifting communal activities.

The gendered domesticity of Ocean Grove, in which the sacred home was presided over by women, inhabited by dutiful children, and frequented by male provider/protectors,[47] suggests that the women here lacked the freedom and authority enjoyed by women in frontier camp meetings or women elsewhere in the holiness movement. But the reality was that evangelical women in general and the women of Ocean Grove in particular never relinquished their roles as exhorters and advocates for social reform (of men). During the latter half of the nineteenth century, numerous women's groups were formed that enabled their pious members to continue the work of bringing conversion and perfection to "lost" society. As the nineteenth century progressed, these women had more and more at stake. Trends in American economy took women out of the production of income, so they were increasingly vulnerable to the loss of family income from male drinking or irresponsibility. If men squandered their earnings at the saloon, women were affected as well. The temperance movement, for example, provided a natural medium for evangelical women's social activism to protect the home against the sins of the father. Epstein argues that women were able to translate the energies they once directed toward converting men to moderating those aspects of male culture most threatening to the home.[48] What began through the efforts primarily of male members of Congregationalist churches to curtail drinking quickly came under female leadership. Noting that the rise of the temperance movement coincided with a per capita decline in the consumption of alcohol, Epstein suggests that the temperance movement provided an opportunity for women to confront a general sense of powerlessness.[49] Estelle Freedman agrees that this and the other public institutions formed by women after 1870 helped mobilize women in the public arena on a range of issues.[50] Evangelical women within the Woman's Christian Temperance Union were able to use the movement as a basis for other relevant social and political causes.[51] For example, in 1903, the women's suffrage meeting and the WCTU gathering were held the same week in Ocean Grove; Bishop Fitzgerald spoke out strongly in favor of suffrage for all and then later greeted the WCTU members to address their cause.[52]

The WCTU, albeit protofeminist, was careful to separate itself from what emerged after 1920 as a campaign for a real and equitable balance of powers between men and women. Freedman credits the effectiveness of the WCTU and other women's institutions of the period with their ability to advocate for women's concerns within a culture that did not challenge the Victorian ideal of "true womanhood."[53] She continues, "Although the women's movement of the late nineteenth century contributed to the transformation of women's social roles it did not reject a separate, unique female identity."[54] The WCTU challenged male sociability out of a concern for the protection of the Christian home, the same concern that provoked the fervent prayers of wives and mothers at the beginning of the nineteenth century. Within this struggle, suffrage was not a means for women to gain access to public office but, rather, for women to defend the home. While men could be counted on to legislate for the benefit of industry, Epstein maintains that Victorian women believed that "only a female electorate would see to it that laws were passed for the protection of the family."[55]

In reality, then, the gendered performances of holiness in Ocean Grove were not incompatible. Men contained their violent impulses through discipline and physical training, women were fit mothers and faithful exhorters, and both were faithful protectors of a model Christian society. The women who spent their leisure hours at Ocean Grove in the company of other women, passionately speaking out against the horrors of liquor and demanding their place at the ballot box, were modeling a vision of themselves as faithful guardians of the sacred home. The male police, trustees, and ushers protected the same home, but from a different place. Stansell suggests that the nineteenth-century reform of New York City's streets was an effort at creating an asylum on a grand scale to embody the virtues of industry and domesticity. To do so meant marking the boundaries of public and private space: "the public space of the metropolis would be the precinct of men, the private space of the home, that of women and children."[56] Ocean Grove was an effort at modeling the Christian home on a community scale. Women were inside—praying, overseeing children's nurture, living in the mutual accountability of an extended parlor meeting, and forming alliances with other women to combat the forces that challenged the sanctity of that home. Men were at the threshold to the exterior world—sober and disciplined, standing guard lest the forces of the world threaten the holiness meeting within. Ocean Grove was not, however, the modeling of just any Christian home. It was the modeling of *the* Christian home—the holy city to come, where the perfect would dwell in the presence of God.

6

JERUSALEM BY THE SEA

And I saw the holy city, the new Jerusalem, coming down out of
heaven from God, prepared as a bride adorned for her husband.
And I heard a loud voice from the throne saying,
  "See, the home of God is among mortals.
  God will dwell with them as their God;
  They will be God's peoples."

Revelation 21:2–3

For the holiness people of Ocean Grove, the promised land was not just "pie in the sky, by and by." The Holy Land was a present possibility on this earth; the perfected were being readied to populate this land through their personal growth in holiness. Claiming the millennial promise that the city of God would appear when a perfected people were ready to inhabit it, the visitors to Ocean Grove modeled themselves as its rightful citizens. Ocean Grove became Jerusalem-by-the-sea—the biblical city at the end of an age, at the beginning of the age to come. Becoming this other place meant performing the Other. The people of the Grove could inhabit the new Jerusalem only insofar as they could place themselves within the Jerusalem of the Holy Land. The modeling of perfection was nowhere more developed than in the performances of holy leisure that made explicit this connection between Ocean Grove and Jerusalem and between Grovers and the Jerusalemites they sought to become.

Situated in the heart of Ocean Grove, at the end of the wide Ocean Pathway that leads directly to the sea, a scale model of nineteenth-century Jerusalem marked the spiritual center for the holiness people of Ocean Grove. The permanent roof built to protect the fragile model still stands today in the shadow of the Great Auditorium. Summer guests to the seaside religious community were led through the streets of this model on "tours" that mimicked tours they might have experienced in the actual nineteenth-century city. Lecturers used the three-dimensional map to illustrate their

Bible lessons. For many years after its construction, the camp-meeting revival concluded with a pilgrimage to "Jerusalem"—the model, that is—in a ritual reenactment of the pilgrimage Ocean Grove residents made each year in hopes of finding the holy city by the sea.

The Gibbonses' history reiterates an account of the origin of this model given in the early annual reports of the camp meeting. They record that the Reverend W. W. Wythe, M. D., a resident of Ocean Grove, built the model "at a great expenditure of time, research, labor and an actual outlay of about $2500 in money. He presented the Model to Ocean Grove in 1881."[1] In actual fact, the Jerusalem model came to Ocean Grove in 1879 from New York City, where "large numbers of visitors had the pleasure to inspect it." The *Ocean Grove Record* states on 12 July 1879 that a "tent to shelter the model arrived and was put up last week."[2] This enclosed tent was located directly across from the association office on Main Avenue at Central Avenue. In 1881, the model was indeed presented to the Ocean Grove Camp Meeting Association and moved to its site near the auditorium. As an official monument of the community, the model became the focus of several important public rituals. Wythe had built the structure on the basis of personal knowledge gained from his travels to Jerusalem. He also had previous experience building at least one other Holy Land model for a religious retreat center.

Modeling As Religious Pedagogy

In 1874, the summer that the Chautauqua Sunday-school assembly grounds opened in upstate New York, Wythe labored meticulously over a model called Palestine Park. Extending 75 by 120 feet, this scale model of the land occupied by the ancient Hebrews bordered Lake Chautauqua and incorporated that shoreline as the Mediterranean coast. Wythe landscaped the area to represent the hills and valleys of Palestine and then added miniature plaster models of the significant cities. Lester Vogel records that the idea for this model came from Chautauqua founder John Heyl Vincent, "who meant to use it to enhance one of his 'visual education' aids."[3] It was based on an earlier prototype that had been attempted in a grove adjacent to Vincent's New Jersey congregation.[4] The model evidently made a considerable impression on many of the early Chautauqua guests, and Vogel records the reactions of two notable attendees who commented on it. Presidential candidate James Garfield remarked of it in 1880, "It has been the struggle of the world to get more leisure, but it was left for Chautauqua to show how to use it." Rudyard Kipling was more skeptical of the work, commenting sardonically after his visit to Chautauqua in 1889 that there were "artificial hillocks surrounding a mud puddle . . . little boulders topped with square pieces of putty were strewn over the hillocks—evidently with intention."[5]

Kipling's comments notwithstanding, Wythe's Palestine Park served a clear and useful purpose in the opinion of Vogel. He maintains, "Although it inspired praise and merriment, the model had a single serious purpose: it was intended for instruction, careful study, and contemplation."[6] Vincent had founded Chautauqua to be a place where Sunday-school teachers could devote themselves to intensive Bible study. By the last quarter of the nineteenth century, Holy Land geography was an essential component of that study, as important as a thorough exegesis of the text itself. Vincent believed so strongly in the ability of Chautauqua's model to aid in this study that he claimed that "an examination of the model in conjunction with the proper text was 'almost equivalent to an actual tour of the Holy Land.'"[7] Vincent's enthusiasm for modeling as a component of Bible study and Wythe's expertise in creating these models were soon felt at Ocean Grove.

With the opening of the Sunday-school assembly in Ocean Grove in 1879, Wythe unveiled the detailed model of Jerusalem on Main Avenue in Ocean Grove. The *Ocean Grove Record* of 9 August 1979 ran both an advertisement and an editorial comment on the structure.[8] The advertisement boasted a "Mammoth Model of Jerusalem," where a "course of four lectures on Jerusalem and the Bible will be delivered by Dr. W. W. Wythe." A single admission to the "lectures" was advertised at twenty-five cents, a course of four lectures for fifty cents, and reserved seats for the course at seventy-five cents. The accompanying article suggested, "No better Bible illustration could be given than one of Dr. Wythe's lectures, delivered daily in connection with the Model." The paper also proposed a Bible class that would meet there every day for study and suggested that one ought to allow a half hour to see it. The author did not mention whether or not the proposed Bible class was the same as the "lectures" advertised for twenty-five cents each.

The enclosed structure and admission price imply that Dr. Wythe's Bible lectures differed from both the Bible study typical of holiness camp meetings and Vincent's practice in Chautauqua. Unlike the open Palestine Park at Chautauqua, upon which Kipling could stumble accidentally, Wythe's Ocean Grove model was first accessible only through paid admission; moreover, references in the advertisement to admission prices suggested the idiom of popular entertainment. Granted, Dr. Wythe was generous to donate a $2,500 structure to the meeting grounds, but if a substantial number of the summer guests from 1879 and 1880 attended one or more of his lectures, he may well have recovered all his initial costs before he gave the model to the Ocean Grove Camp Meeting Association.

Figure 23. The Jerusalem pavilion as it still stands today before the auditorium. Photograph by Troy Messenger.

As was the case with so much of Ocean Grove, Wythe's "mammoth" model and enlightening presentations of Jerusalem, entertaining as they might be, were acceptable only insofar as they were construed to be holy leisure that could lead the individual and community toward perfection. The model was indeed used for Bible study; but it must also be seen in light of nineteenth-century performance of museum lectures and the role of these lectures as moral entertainment. The antipathy of Protestant culture toward the theatre since the time of the Reformation was still strong in the nineteenth century.[9] Museums, on the other hand, were able to reframe performances that would otherwise have been objectionable to religious conservatives, presenting these performances as morally acceptable science or education.[10] Neil Harris, for example, suggests that P. T. Barnum succeeded largely because he capitalized on conservative Protestants' willingness to view entertainment as education. Harris says, "Museum lecture rooms . . . were not theaters but could do what theaters did: mount dramatic entertainments or present variety acts under the guise of education and public enlightenment."[11] The baptism of these performances as a means of growth in holiness granted Grovers permission to marvel over the model's detail and enjoy engaging lecturers.

Dr. Wythe's model benefited not only from this Christian approval of lectures and "museum performance" but also from the overwhelming American interest in anything connected with the Holy Land. Although the popularity of the Holy Land was peaking in the 1870s and 1880s, even in the early days of American Methodism, the locale was already present in the popular language of the denomination.[12] Richey records that, in the eighteenth century, Methodists commonly spoke of Zion to "evoke both historical Israel and the eschatological New Jerusalem." Richey notes that the richly evocative symbolism of Zion language "identified Methodism with the people of God, the corporate, transcongregational reality of God's chosen ones."[13] This image of Zion was indeed common in the vernacular of Ocean Grove. The painted text above the speakers' platform in the second auditorium was a paraphrase of Hebrews 12:22–24:

> But ye are come unto mount Zion, and unto the *city of the living God, the heavenly Jerusalem,* and to an innumerable company of angels, to the general assembly and Church of the first born, which are written in heaven, and to God the Judge of all, and to the spirits of just men made *perfect,* and to Jesus the mediator of *the new covenant, and to the blood of sprinkling* that speaketh better things than that of Abel.[14]

This appropriation of Zion by nineteenth-century Christian America whetted an appetite for knowledge of the actual Holy Land. The midcentury interest in "scriptural geography" based on firsthand observation of Palestine is an example of this trend. Driven by a need to counter evidence emerging from the new field of geology that contradicted biblical accounts of the age of the world, nineteenth-century biblical scholarship moved from an exegesis based on text alone to an observation of the actual landscape of that text. Union Seminary professor Edward Robinson, known as "the greatest master of measuring tape in the world," actually went around the walls of Jerusalem with a 100-foot measuring tape.[15]

The same interest was expressed in the increasing popularity of the country of Palestine as a tourist/pilgrimage site. Known as the Holy Land because of its identification with the land of Jesus' ministry and ancient Israel, Palestine had been a dangerous and impractical destination for all except the most adventurous Westerner prior to the Egyptian conquest of Syria in 1831. However, with the relative peace under Egyptian control, scholars, clergy, artists, and eventually pleasure seekers from the West began to visit the Holy Land in ever-increasing numbers.[16] Western travelers in the 1850s and 1860s still depended on the services—erratic at best—of native guides called dragomen, and could expect the occasional crowd of rock-throwing natives.[17] In the postbellum years, American pilgrimage to the Holy Land expanded rapidly and quickly merged with a burgeoning tourist industry catering to such travel. In 1867, Henry Ward Beecher's church organized a "pleasure trip" of 150 Americans to the Holy Land and Egypt. The trip is described satirically by one of the participants, the young humorist Mark Twain, in *The Innocents Abroad*.[18]

In 1869, the year of Ocean Grove's founding, Cook's Eastern Tours paved the way for a new style of tourism to the Holy Land. These tours made the pilgrimage tolerable for an increasingly sophisticated class of Western tourists, offering English food, handpicked dragomen, hassle-free passage through customs, guaranteed accommodations, and a fixed price. Between 1868 and 1882, Cook hosted 4,200 pilgrims, who were able to use their hymn books and Bibles at every turn. Naomi Shepherd notes that it "was easier to be a working man travelling with Cook than an unbeliever. . . . The guides used every opportunity to provide biblical illustrations, and the tourists could not pass through a wicket gate without hearing reflections on the strait gate of the Gospels."[19] Tourists seeking a spiritual experience with the Holy Land expected guides to be part lecturer/part preacher.

For those who could not make the arduous journey to the Middle East, the Holy Land was brought to them in the form of copious diaries, travelogues, geographies, guides, and even printed sermons on the area, most lavishly illustrated with drawings, engravings, watercolors, and photographs. Hundreds of monographs on Palestine appeared. In America, the most popular book after *Uncle Tom's Cabin* was William Thomson's *Land and the Book*. In France, Ernest Renan's *Vie de Jésus*, a highly romantic critique of the Gospels based on a two-month trip to Palestine in 1861, became the most read book after the Bible. Shepherd maintains:

> By 1854, wrote one weary reviewer in the *British Art Journal* of a book by a missionary's wife, "the subject has been gone over again and again, until the Holy Land is better known in England than the English Lakes." Protestant hymns became explicitly geographical; the huge family bibles were illustrated with a combination of Renaissance reproductions, archaeological diagrams from Egyptian excavations, and prints copied from travel memoirs.[20]

There seemed to be no end of Holy Land material to feed the insatiable appetite of evangelicals for the landscape of their faith.

The increased access in the nineteenth century to the actual sites produced a proliferation of models that sought to re-create parts of the Holy Land in the West. In 1833, a party of English architects and draftsmen set out to make detailed drawings of the city. Robert Burford, the London impresario who ran the Leicester Square Pavilion, used these sketches to stage the

"Panorama of Jerusalem" in 1836. The murals of Jerusalem were hung in a huge rotunda covering ten thousand square feet, and costumed performers entertained one hundred forty thousand people there in what was convincing "evidence of popular interest in Palestine which was to continue undiminished throughout the century."[21]

If Burford's extravagant panorama marked the beginning of this new period of modeling the Holy Land, the equally impressive exhibit of Jerusalem at the 1904 St. Louis World's Fair came toward the end.[22] The St. Louis model was a ten-acre reproduction of the principal features and life of Jerusalem. The site was contoured to replicate the Jerusalem landscape, and inside the walls were life-size re-creations of significant buildings— the Church of the Holy Sepulcher, Temple Mount, Solomon's Stables, the Golden Gates, Via Dolorosa, and the Wailing Wall. The narrow streets were peopled with native "Jerusalemites" and livestock. Religious services were staged as pageants.

Like Burford's, this exhibit was created by someone with firsthand knowledge of the actual city. Rev. W. B. Palmore, who directed the project, had traveled to Palestine several times.[23] Rev. E. Morris Ferguson, general secretary of the New Jersey Sunday School Association, gave a revealing account of how this model was received. Echoing Vincent's words spoken thirty-five years earlier, he encouraged those who could not attend the World Convention held that year in the real Jerusalem to view this exhibit, because it was of equal educational and spiritual value. "It is a remarkable fact that Palestine has changed little since the days of Christ, and in some respects but little, if any, since the days of Abraham."[24] Given that nineteenth-century Jerusalem and its people bore little resemblance to the first-century city and its citizenry, such a claim is astounding.

The fascination of nineteenth-century Christians with Palestine and with Jerusalem in particular was replicated in Ocean Grove. Hymnody, worship, Bible teaching, leisure reading, architecture, and popular entertainment all made reference to the Holy Land. In worship, Grovers sang,

> Jerusalem the golden,
>   With milk and honey blest,
> Beneath thy contemplation
>   Sink heart and voice oppressed.
>
> I know not, O I know not
>   What joys await us there,
> What radiancy of glory,
>   What bliss beyond compare.[25]

The *Ocean Grove Record,* in an 1879 article called "Pilgrimages to Jerusalem," reported "vast migrations" every spring to Jerusalem. The author claims that, if this were hindered, it would lead to a "modern day crusade. . . . It is a true pilgrimage of faith, the one event in a life of dull monotony and sordid cares, the one ecstasy of poetry in an existence of poverty and ignorance."[26] Those who could not visit Jerusalem in person did so vicariously, through the photographs and "oriental" objects that pilgrims brought back from the Holy City. In 1880, the *Ocean Grove Record* ran an advertisement for an exhibit and bazaar featuring "2000 sq. ft. of surface and showing every edifice, public and private in the city, also a panorama of the holy city covering 2500 sq. ft. of canvas. Admission including printed description and map, 10¢. The oriental bazaar will be found in connection with a full line of beautiful Eastern goods."[27] This exhibit was staged concurrently with Wythe's model and lectures. The following year, Dr. James Strong of Drew Seminary gave a lecture titled "All Around Jerusalem," accompanied by photographic views (presented by stereopticon). The article reporting this lecture claimed that people visiting Ocean Grove had "most of the advantages of friends visiting the Middle East," from Dan to Beersheba, without the "inconveniences" of the sun and caravans.[28]

In the midst of this flurry of Holy Land performances at Ocean Grove, the annual report of the Camp Meeting Association records that Wythe spent not only $2,500 but also "a vast amount of careful thought, and historical research" to build an *accurate* replica of late nineteenth-century Jerusalem.[29] Wythe constructed the model from his own extensive firsthand interaction with the city. His accuracy was verified by the tourist/pilgrims who had been to Palestine. Their testimony is cited in each account of the model:

> This beautiful, and according to the united testimony of all oriental travelers who have seen it, singularly correct and perfect structure . . .[30]

> So accurate is the reproduction that scores of travelers who have visited Jerusalem have found delight in identifying its different sections and even individual buildings.[31]

> The highest testimonials have been given by the secular and religious press throughout the country as well as by hundreds of eminent divines and travelers.[32]

In order to be useful in religious pedagogy, the model had to be an accurate representation, as well as being large and detailed.

Systematic study of the Bible, essential to the pursuit of perfection, was a regular component of everyday life at the mature camp meetings like Ocean

Grove. Throughout the summer, individual study, gatherings in small groups, and lectures by Bible teachers alternated with other daily meetings for prayer, worship, and preaching. Wythe's model quickly became the preferred audio-visual aid—the ultimate three-dimensional reference map—to accompany the daily round of Bible instruction.

John Davis records an example of this mode of biblical teaching based on Holy Land models. Vincent developed a Sunday-school curriculum that used Palestine Park at Chautauqua and that was based on learning through an imagined visit to Palestine. "The very means of instruction often served to create an artificial sense of having experienced the Holy Land terrain."[33] The method included pretending to write letters home from Palestine, and "classed pupils at progressive levels, depending on their increasing knowledge of Palestine: 'Pilgrims to the Holy Land, Resident in Palestine, Dweller in Jerusalem, Explorer of Bible Lands, and Templar.'"[34]

Vincent taught the Bible by replicating popular Holy Land tourist excursions, such as those led by Cook. These tours were, after all, a form of Bible study, for evangelical Americans used their travels as a way to verify and elucidate biblical stories. Biblical scholars like Horatio Hackett used observation of nineteenth-century houses in Jaffa to exegete Peter's vision on a housetop.[35] William C. Prime, a layman who wrote an account of his travels to the Holy Land in 1855–1856, commented at the end of his travels, "The Bible was a new book, faith in which seemed now to have passed into actual sight, and every page of its record shone out with new, and a thousand-fold increased lustre."[36] Scores of nineteenth-century authors attributed visits to Palestine with a fresh understanding of biblical texts. Conversely, these pilgrims always experienced the land through the lens of sacred stories, which recast the people, buildings, and landscape of nineteenth-century Palestine as participants in a timeless biblical drama.

The model of Jerusalem allowed Ocean Grove guests to engage in the same mode of Bible study used by tourists to both the actual Palestine and Vincent's modeled Palestine. In Ocean Grove, lecturers "led" people through important sites in Jerusalem as if the listeners were tourist/pilgrims to the city itself. Allen Moore's *Modern City of Jerusalem As Shown by Wythe's Great Model of the Holy City* is a written "tour" and an excellent example of this mode of teaching. This undated pamphlet probably was printed in the first quarter of the twentieth century, sometime after the first lectures given at the model. Because it appears to be either a script for an oral presentation or a transcription, it sheds important light on the tradition of oral performances that occurred at Ocean Grove. The Gibbonses record that Moore was one of the lecturers at the model.[37] And the *Ocean Grove Times* reports that, in addition to these lectures, Moore presented a "Palestine Exposition" in St. Paul's Church of Ocean Grove in July 1912.[38] Moore's "site-seeing" mode of study/performance is consistent with the nineteenth-century tradition of exhibiting foreign lands. Barbara Kirshenblatt-Gimblett argues that "the experience of travel became the model for exhibitions about other places" and that the exhibitions were presented as "a surrogate for travel."[39] Indeed, Moore's text invites visitors to experience the model by imagining themselves as travelers within it.

Moore intersperses biblical prophecies with archaeological scholarship and "points of interest." The pamphlet repeatedly reminds the reader of biblical texts that prophesy the current state of Jerusalem. The city was not portrayed in its first-century form, even though that might better illustrate the New Testament passages. Instead, its contemporary form was shown to validate biblical prophecy, thereby underscoring the reliability of the Bible. The fulfillment of prophecy in Jerusalem thus provided a basis for reconciling discrepancies between what the Bible described and what travelers could see, as well as for the teaching and acceptance of other biblical prophecies.

Moore's text/performance first situates Jerusalem in its surrounding landscape and then guides the spectator through the sites of New Testament events. However, the description of these biblical-era events places them within the contemporary city. The simultaneous presentation of ancient event and contemporary place would have been analogous to nineteenth-century pilgrimage tours through Jerusalem. For example, the place where Jesus stood before Pilate is marked with the Arch Ecce Homo in front of the Convent of the Sisters of Zion. Below this building is the place of Jesus' judgment, and leading away from it is the crooked street known as the Via Dolorosa. The point on this route where Jesus is said to have fallen under the weight of the cross is marked by the Austrian Hospice "for entertainment of pilgrims from that country."

Accompanying this travelogue is an introduction to scholarly debates surrounding archaeological and historical evidence. Moore explains the "difference of opinion among scholars as to the true site of Calvary," noting that insufficient evidence exists to substantiate either proposed site but judging the practice of "Holy Fire" at the Chapel of the Sepulcher sufficient to discredit that site. Despite the arbitrariness implied in this instance, Moore's interest in the specificity of location of the biblical events is based on firsthand investigation of the streets of Jerusalem as well as familiarity with current scholarship surrounding its excavation. He is doing biblical scholarship in the same manner as the Protestant scholars of the nineteenth century—that is, by comparing geographic evidence based on fieldwork at the site with the biblical text. His introduction to the model, probably written in the first quarter of the twentieth century, reads like many of the monographs produced by visitors who toured Jerusalem in the nineteenth century. For Moore, Bible study required access to place as well as text. He says, "These excavations are watched with great interest by Biblical scholars."[40] Moreover, Jerusalem—the Christian center of the Holy Land because of Jesus' crucifixion and resurrection there—was preeminently important among the sites of biblical events.

Accounts of travel experiences like those of Moore's lecture/pamphlet were a paradigm that shaped performance vis-à-vis the Holy Land. The printed sermons of T. DeWitt Talmage demonstrate that such pious travelogues existed simultaneously as both oral and written performance. Upon returning from the Holy Land, Talmage preached a series of sermons based on his experience. Printed editions of these became bestsellers in both America and Europe.[41] His published sermon "Jerusalem the Golden" follows the familiar model. For example, he first went to the site of Calvary, being careful to document the controversy over the location and why he preferred the nontraditional site outside the city walls. The skull-shaped hill confirmed for him the accuracy of the biblical witness, for Golgotha was the "place of a skull." The biblical stories of Jerusalem provided an itinerary for his stay in the city, and the city provided fresh material to animate those stories.

Talmage's sermon reveals that the nineteenth-century evangelical attraction to the Holy Land went beyond its utility in authenticating and interpreting the Bible. In them, he vividly recalled the emotions that brought him to tears as he read the sacred texts associated with Jerusalem. Although he noted the disparity between what he actually saw in the city and his image of the religious reality of Jerusalem, this disparity only occasioned an exhortation that the faithful launch

> a crusade of Gospel Peace! . . . and Jerusalem, purified of all its idolatries, and taking back the Christ she once cast out, shall be made a worthy type of that heavenly city which Paul styled "the mother of us all," and which St. John saw, "the holy Jerusalem descending out of heaven from God." Through its gates may we all enter when our work is done, and in its temple, greater than all the earthly temples piled in one, may we worship.[42]

Implied in this move from the actual to the spiritual, from the earthly to the heavenly Jerusalem, is an interest in the Holy Land that goes beyond either education or even entertainment couched as education. Contrary to Lester Vogel's assertion that the Holy Land model at Chautauqua was soley an aid

Figure 24. Jerusalem as depicted in the annual report of 1881. Reprinted from the *Ocean Grove Annual Report,* 1881, 22.

in religious education, the model of Jerusalem at Ocean Grove modeled on many levels at once. Study of Scripture through the Holy Land (real or modeled) was not a dispassionate science for Christian pilgrims like Talmage. Evangelical Christians in the Holy Land were people of faith, and Jerusalem was the sacred center of that faith. The model of Jerusalem was not only a means for learning but also a way to touch that sacred center, walk its streets, and become its rightful citizens.

Modeling As Protestant Iconography

For the holiness seekers who fervently desired to be at this sacred center, the model was more than a useful didactic tool. It was a way to go to Jerusalem— to be in the Holy Land and, by extension, to be holy. For those who could not make a pilgrimage, the model provided iconic access to the sacred center of faith. Jerusalem was no longer in the Middle East; it had come to the Jersey shore.

In the annual report of 1881, the text described the newly situated model of Jerusalem next to the auditorium in Ocean Grove, but illustrated this text with a glorious city on a hill. In the illustration, visitors to the Ocean Grove model have become Holy Land pilgrims riding camels and wearing long robelike garments. This leap across time and space was common in representations of the "land of the Bible" for nineteenth-century America. Israel was "understood as the people of the *biblical* nation, and, by extension, the land they inhabited"[43] [emphasis mine]. This created an oddly distorted narrative of place. The landscape painted by nineteenth-century artists was an idealized rendering of the contemporary topographical features and buildings, while the people depicted were usually attired somewhere between the burnous and the toga."[44] In this illustration of the people of Ocean Grove making a pilgrimage to the model of Jerusalem, the subjects have been transported out of the landscape and dress of Ocean Grove and into a quasi-biblical landscape and, by extension, into a biblical narrative. This process reveals how the model symbolically transported viewers to a holy time and place, enabling them to merge their own sacred history with the sacred history of Jerusalem. The illustration of the model of Jerusalem in the annual report could just as well have been used to illustrate Jerusalem for the family Bible.

Nineteenth-century illustrators of the Bible invariably represented Palestine as the Palestine of faith. The English painter David Wilkie, who visited the Holy Land in 1841, was widely influential in his belief that "biblical painters should first acquire as much knowledge as they could about their subject, then discard whatever was incongruous to the Western eye."[45] Shepherd observes, "No artist, professional or amateur, who visited Palestine ever attempted to show the poverty, dirt and commercial exploitation of the Holy Places described by every visitor."[46] Because late-nineteenth-century photography required long exposures, photographers posed models in idealized tableaux vivants to create images that resembled a "museum exhibit."[47] Images in Bibles, monographs, and stereographs fed America's hunger for the "real" Holy Land: the closer the artist to the sacred place, the closer the viewers of his or her images to the sacred. The interaction of the artist with the place and people—through the "eyes of faith"—provided the possibility of a similar interaction of the viewer with the subject. John Davis maintains, "To an increased degree, they were experienced as 'co-substantial' with the sacred objects."[48] In the process of being annexed to the Bible, the photographs became objects of veneration themselves.

The annual report of 1891 shows that Ocean Grove's model of Jerusalem was viewed with the same reverence as other Biblical illustrations.

> As Jerusalem of old is the Christian sacred city, and more Christian people sigh to behold it than any other in the world, so this model, like a picture, being its exact representation, is gazed at from year to year, with a reverence in many instances amounting almost to awe.[49]

The experience of "awe" at a visual representation of the holy sounds distinctly un-Protestant. But because the model was an "exact" representation, to visit it was somehow to visit the real city, not just because it was the educational equivalent but because it was also the spiritual equivalent. This icon, in an iconoclastic branch of Christianity, resembled icons in the medieval church in that its accurate representation of a symbolic archetype guaranteed access to the original.

With their physical materials and simulated landscapes, Holy Land models blurred the distinction between model and archetype in a way that photographs could not.[50] Davis records that Palestine Park incorporated "relics" such as Middle Eastern soil, bits of stone and wood, and other objects taken from Palestine. Visitors to Chautauqua could even take blades of grass from the model, in much the same way they would have taken cherished objects from Palestine itself.[51] The material rendering of the sacred provided a direct, iconic link between the model and the real. Yet the miniaturization process removed the inhabitants, leaving an idealized Palestine of faith, what Davis describes as "purified and miniaturized, rid of the problematic elements that compromised a visit to the actual Holy Land."[52] Kirshenblatt-Gimblett notes that modeling through miniaturization is a way of freezing an image of a time and place within a "hermetic universe, autonomous and controllable."[53] Within this perfect world, people are often missing. Dollhouses, for example, often have no dolls, so their owners can put themselves in the house.[54] Likewise, Ocean Grove's Jerusalem, perfected and depopulated through miniaturization, was ready to be repopulated by the people of Ocean Grove.

In Moore's lecture, we not only hear the scholarly debate surrounding the location of historical events but we are also invited to place ourselves before God at the Holy of Holies, touch the stones placed by Solomon, and walk with Jesus down the Via Dolorosa. When performed at the model city, the tourist/pilgrimage procession inscribes meaning into place. What Louis Marin describes in parades also holds true in this procession from site to site, where "moving through these named places, re-enacts a myth, legend, or story."[55] The model of the modern city became an icon that could, through performance, provide access to the holy. In lectures at Ocean Grove, a narrative of sites led pilgrims through a mental procession that was functionally analogous to actually proceeding through the streets of Jerusalem.

The Gibbonses encourage guests to the Grove to visit Jerusalem *by visiting the model.* "Christians may obtain first hand information on the City of our Savior by visiting the model *in this religious mecca*"[56] [emphasis mine]. By the late nineteenth century, it had in fact become a religious duty to make a pilgrimage to the Christian equivalent of Mecca—if not to Palestine

Figure 25. In this late nineteenth-century postcard, the Model of Jerusalem does not yet have its protective covering. Note the dozens of miniature trees and rolling landscape. Reprinted from a souvenir postcard of the Historical Society of Ocean Grove. Courtesy of the Ocean Grove Historical Society.

itself then to one of the many models that proliferated as panoramas, landscapes, and environmental theatre. Davis quotes an enthusiastic pilgrim:

> "We are just returned from 'a pilgrimage to the Holy Land' with an admiring company of Bible Christians. . . . Mahomet enjoined upon his followers the duty of making a pilgrimage to Mecca once, at least, in their lives—we consider it quite as much a duty for every Christian, who has it in his power, to visit an exhibition that they will find far less laborious, but not a whit less interesting, instructive, or binding."[57]

The ambiguity of place in the Gibbonses' exhortation to come to this "religious Mecca" reveals how blurred the lines were between the model, Ocean Grove, Jerusalem in the Middle East, and the heavenly Jerusalem. Where exactly was "this religious Mecca"? Ocean Grove or Jerusalem? The model was in Ocean Grove, but the Mecca of Jewish and Christian faith was Jerusalem. Or was it, for these millenarian Methodists, the new holy city on the Jersey shore where thousands of them made a yearly pilgrimage? Iconically, the difference did not matter—just as praying to a saint counted as praying to an icon of the saint; just as Talmage could look at the squalid city of Jerusalem and see the heavenly city of the millennium; just as Zion was simultaneously in Palestine, Zion the model, Zion as Ocean Grove, and Zion of heavenly promise. In a pilgrimage to Ocean Grove, the faithful could dwell simultaneously in the biblical Jerusalem and the sanctified Jerusalem of the coming age. Not surprisingly, one of the favorite hymns composed in Ocean Grove was "Beulah Land."

> O Beulah Land, sweet Beulah Land
>   As on thy highest mountain I stand,
> I look away across the sea,
>   Where mansions are prepared for me,
> And view the shining glory shore,
>   My heav'n, my home, for evermore![58]

Modeling As Ethnology

The *Ocean Grove Record* headline proudly proclaimed on 25 August 1883 "Another Great Day in Zion," and the article that followed reported on a surf meeting the previous Sunday evening. Because Dr. Stokes had forgotten to ask people beforehand to be prepared to "testify," the testimonies were perhaps more spontaneous than usual. After several people spoke, "Miss Von Finklestein, a native of Jerusalem, standing in the outer circle near the sea, recalled the first surf meeting instituted by the blessed Jesus, on the shore of the sea of Galilee. . . . There were 5,000 converted in one day in her native city once, and we have the same Christ and the same power."[59]

One week later, the camp meeting held its traditional love feast. This service, typically scheduled near the close of a camp meeting, officially welcomed the newly converted into the church.[60] It began with singing and then moved to testimonies, many of which were reported in the newspapers. There were at least two notable attendees at the 1883 love feast at Ocean Grove—the renowned hymn writer Fannie Crosby and Lydia Von Finklestein. Allusions to Zion and the New Jerusalem were scattered throughout the testimonies. One young man described his new spiritual state as having a "certificate of citizenship to the new Jerusalem. . . . Miss Von Finklestein said the allusions she heard to Jerusalem roused her memories of the sacred city where she was born. As the tribes used to go up there, so the people come here, to get ready for the spiritual Zion. She belonged to that band—hallelujah!"[61]

On Labor Day afternoon, immediately after the close of the camp meeting, Von Finklestein did indeed return to Jerusalem—to the model, that is—to give a farewell performance.

> At the model, with rod in hand, she pointed out many places of interest in the city, and described the customs and daily life of Syrian people, to an audience of several hundred persons, who crowded around the

circle. All were delighted not only with the lecture, but with the lecturer, who during her sojourn among us has won many friends. We can heartily reciprocate her closing words: "Farewell, and should we never meet again on earth may we recognize each other in the new Jerusalem whither we are journeying." Miss Von Finklestein returns to New York this week and will soon commence a lecture tour. We understand that she intends revisiting Jerusalem with her brother next spring.[62]

These revealing accounts of Von Finklestein, whose stay in Ocean Grove coincided with both the early years of the model and America's infatuation with the Holy Land, underscore the multiple layers of the performance of Jerusalem at Ocean Grove. She stood at the model, "rod in hand," didactically illustrating the significant locations of biblical events. Her preference for oriental costume and obvious performance competence in the illustrated-lecture style also provided edifying entertainment at this religious seaside resort. But she is probably most significant as evidence of the community's use of performed ethnology of Middle Eastern people to model perfection.

With his trips to the Holy Land, Edward Robinson practiced not only scriptural geography but also what might be called "scriptural ethnology." He regarded the people he encountered as "living illustrations" who could authenticate the sacred writings.[63] Late-nineteenth-century books on Palestine referred not only to topography and architecture but also to how the current residents of these landscapes and their everyday life shed light on ancient texts. Kirshenblatt-Gimblett documents this nineteenth-century fascination with the people of a place in the numerous museum displays that incorporated humans in cultural displays.[64] Although these people sometimes staged important rituals or cultural performances, often they performed the "quotidian as spectacle."[65]

Costumed performers frequently complemented Holy Land exhibits. Yet the Palestinian life these performers portrayed to illuminate the Bible was an amorphous collection of practices from several different cultures in the Holy Land—Jewish, Christian, and Arab. Accompanying these Holy Land performances were numerous exhibitions of living Jews and Jewish culture, most of which reflected an obvious uncertainty about how to portray the subject. Although the "Exposition of the Jews of Many Lands" in Cincinnati in 1913 successfully conveyed the heterogeneity of Jewish culture throughout twenty-seven countries, other exhibits struggled with whether to represent Jews as a unified biblical culture or some amalgam of Jews in Western countries.[66]

For American evangelicals, the Jews in their cities were of much less interest than the ancient biblical people of Palestine who could authenticate their Christian scriptures. But who and where were the people of the Bible? In actual fact, the current residents of Palestine were not the Jews of Jesus' time. Shepherd describes the problem Jewish inhabitants of the Holy Land posed for scholars and artists. She claims, "The Ashkenazi Jews dressed like Polish noblemen of centuries earlier, and kept to their European habits, while the Sefardi Jews, who looked suitably Oriental, had nothing in common with their warlike and agrarian ancestors."[67] By midcentury, the Bedouins, who had often been used as models for the illustrations of biblical patriarchs in family Bibles, were no longer acceptable as "contemporary illustrations."[68] But if the Bedouins and Jews were eliminated, that left only the Moslem peasantry as heirs to the people and customs of the Bible.[69] In an odd cultural turn, "oriental life"—the customs and rituals of everyday peasant life—became a means for American Protestants to understand the Bible. They believed these living customs, like the enduring landscape, provided access to the time of Christ and, thus, to Christ himself. The performance of these customs and rituals *in America,* often by people with no Palestinian background, was an effort to transport this proximity to the holy through performed ethnology.

In 1884, Miss Von Finkelstein and her brother Peter returned to Ocean Grove. At the end of the summer, they participated in a series of extremely popular performances that portrayed contemporary everyday life in their native land as a "realistic illustration of many passages" of scripture.

> FRIDAY, Aug. 8— . . . The mere two-line announcement we gave of Miss Von Finklestein's lecture filled the Auditorium at 7:30. The front of the platform, with pulpit removed, presented the appearance of a Bedouin camp, and as a daughter of the desert, her own make-up was startlingly picturesque. Peter, her handsome brother, with other attendants, formed the background, and frequently participated in the graphic details which the lecturer gave of Arab life, from early Bible times down to the period when these delightful personages themselves roamed the hills and valleys "beyond Jordan." Peter frequently flourished a dangerous looking scimitar, to the admiration of the small boys, and terror of nervous old ladies who, in what they saw and heard, had a realistic illustration of many passages familiar to them in the Scriptures. . . .

> SATURDAY, Aug. 9— . . . This time the subject was "Peasant Life in Palestine," and the platform presented the characteristics of a rural home, which she described in her usually fluent and graceful manner, commencing with an interesting account of herself and father's family, and how it occurred that of Russian parentage she was born in the sacred city of Jerusalem. . . .

TUESDAY, Aug. 12—Mr. Peter Von Finklestein, dressed as a Turk, delivered another interesting lecture, attended by large crowds at the
Model of Jerusalem.[70]

The incongruity of a scimitar-wielding Arab, rural peasant home life, and a
Turkish tourist guide leading pilgrims through Jerusalem illustrates how
readily contemporary Palestine was appropriated for an imagined relevance
to ancient Jewish life. Although the Von Finklesteins were born in Palestine,
their Russian ancestry and residence in America further complicated this
mixture of cultures and times.

John Davis claims that, in the nineteenth century, "the Holy Land went
through a process of localization and became American."[71] The extensive
familiarity with the area fostered by numerous educational and tourist expeditions led to the belief that Americans' "superior knowledge" of the land
gave them a claim to it. Davis suggests that when the land's contemporary
inhabitants "ultimately failed to measure up to their scriptural forebears,
their American contemporaries were quite happy to step in and assume the
mantle of the chosen people."[72] If the current inhabitants of the Holy Land
did not "measure up" morally or socially in the eyes of evangelicals, their
customs nonetheless provided a link to biblical people. Americans were
indeed willing to "assume the mantle of the chosen people," and they did so
by performing the everyday life of nineteenth-century inhabitants of the
Holy Land.

Oriental theater was frequently performed on the makeshift stages of
Holy Land models. Davis shows that the practice took several forms at
Wythe's model in Chautauqua. Bible lecturers, such as Rev. J. S. Ostrander,
wore "the miter, robe, and breastplate of the high priest."[73] A. O. Van
Lennep, who was born in the Middle East, donned Arabic dress and
"climbed to the top of Chautauqua's 'Oriental House' each day to sing the
call to prayer of an Islamic muezzin."[74] But there were also community
spectacles like the "oriental funeral service" of 1876, in which residents in-
dulged their own fantasies of becoming Holy Land people.[75] One illustration from 1879 shows several people gathered at the model in turbans and
striped robes.

Moore's "Palestine Exposition" staged contemporary "orientals" at Ocean
Grove in 1912. The account of the exhibition in the *Ocean Grove Times* indicates that it lasted for several weeks and required the entire floor space of
St. Paul's Methodist Church. Fifty costumed performers modeled contemporary life in Palestine, while simultaneously performing "biblical" manners,
customs, and costumes. The *Ocean Grove Times* records:

Figure 26. Peter Von Finklestein as he appeared for a series of three lectures to the 1889 Sunday School Assembly in Ocean Grove. Reprinted from the *Ocean Grove Annual Report*, 1889, 51.

Embodied in the display will be Bible manners, customs, costumes, implements, furniture and music, together with Ishmael tent life, Palestine city life and Palestine peasant life.

Fifty trained people in genuine oriental dress will assist Rev. Allen Moore, F.R.G.S., and these will appear in the realistic costume, lectures, the tableaux, the bridal procession, the wedding ceremony, and other interesting ceremonies of the far East. Admission to opening was by offering, exposition and descriptions 10¢, and costume lectures and tableaux 10¢, and to the tabernacle model and lecture 5¢.[76]

Like the Von Finklesteins, these performers moved freely between "interesting ceremonies of the far East" and "Bible manners." Here, however, "trained" Americans stood in for the people of the Holy Land. The exhibition allowed Ocean Grovers the opportunity to try out being people of the Bible by performing contemporary Palestinian life.

For nineteenth-century American evangelicals, the supposed accuracy of these models, lectures, and cultural performances guaranteed accurate knowledge of Bible events and prophecies, a place and its people, Jerusalem and the Jews. It was a way of doing Jewish ethnology in the service of Christianity. Significantly, Moore's text begins and ends with just how many Jews were currently living in Jerusalem. The first paragraph notes that the city "contains about 90,000 inhabitants, of which 60,000 are Jews"; the last paragraph confirms that "a century ago only 300 Jews were allowed permission to reside in the Holy City. . . . In 1875 there were only 13,000 Jews in Jerusalem; now about 60,000." Jerusalem had once again become the city of Jews, as it had been in the days of Jesus. The intervening years of the Diaspora were a minor glitch in the biblical history presented in this model. Davis argues:

> Such playacting bespeaks more than an obvious insensitivity to cultural difference. Its very outlandishness indicates an apparently sincere attempt to "become" the people of the Bible, to move, if only temporarily, from their American status as a metaphorical chosen race in the New World to the actual favored nation of the Old. In this ahistorical conflation of Jewish and Islamic culture, religious and present time, and semitic and Nordic civilization, the "Chosen People" with which they identified became an indistinct Middle Eastern amalgam, a "Bible people" rather than a kingdom of Jews, a nebulous merging of separate cultures almost entirely divorced from contemporary, or even scriptural "reality."[77]

Underscoring this identification of Jerusalem with a fantasized first-century Jew was Lydia Von Finklestein, "herself a native of Jerusalem."[78] She was an icon of the perfected Jew, who transformed the model of Jerusalem into a living diorama.

This kind of performed ethnology was a means of remaking and perfecting the people of Ocean Grove. The blurring of distinctions between nineteenth-century evangelicals, contemporary Arabs and Jews living in Palestine, and fictionalized biblical Jews was what Davis calls "regenerative role-playing."[79] Linking the self to the perfected citizens of Jerusalem (either the biblical or heavenly one) authenticated the individual in the face of a dehumanizing industrial society. Modeling Jews/Jerusalem was part of the larger process of modeling that transformed each performance of everyday life at Ocean Grove into a signifier of the model self. Christianity sprang from Judaism, so in order to understand the pivotal events of the faith, one needed to know the Jewish place where they occurred. To understand the Christian self, one had to know the Jew. But not just any Jew. When separated from the Holy Land of Jewish biblical history, the Jew, according to this line of thinking, became less a Jew. Jewishness was permanently linked with the promised land. Jews in Bradley Beach were of far less interest than a "native of Jerusalem." Any connection with the Holy Land—from restored performances of "interesting ceremonies" to costumed former citizens of Jerusalem leading tourists through modeled streets—transported the nineteenth-century Methodists of Ocean Grove geographically, ethnically, and temporally to their "true" home in the Holy City.

Marching to Zion

Von Finklestein's farewell performance at the model of Jerusalem was not the only event at that site on the closing day of camp meeting in 1883. Nowhere is the iconic function of this model better dramatized than in the annual "March around Jerusalem." For many years, at the end of the final service of the season, a procession filed out of the Great Auditorium and then stopped at each station where religious meetings had been held throughout the summer. Daniels records that on the morning of the last day of camp meeting, the crowd gathered in the auditorium to hear reports on the success of the various meetings. Following the reports, a line formed for the march. The youth choir led the procession, followed by association officers and members, and then by those who were workers or worshipers in the services. Others waited in the auditorium or in the buildings along the procession route. Upon leaving the auditorium, the choir began to sing:

> We're marching to Zion,
> Beautiful, beautiful Zion,
> We're marching upward to Zion,
> That beautiful city of God. (*OGS*, 167)

The procession wound first through the tabernacle, where it stopped for a short prayer of thanksgiving for the success of the services held there. Then the group marched to Thornley Chapel, where the children had been meeting throughout the season. From there the marchers crossed Centennial Park to the Young People's Temple. Daniels continues, "Then out of the Temple and across Ocean Pathway, the line proceeds actually to Jerusalem (The Model), which is circled by the marchers, who still sing the marching hymn." Daniels notes that when the procession returned to the auditorium, "the strains of the hymn are taken up by the great organ, the marchers, those who had waited for their return, and many more who crowded in to be present at the simple but impressive closing ceremony, so well known to hundreds of thousands of frequenters of Ocean Grove during the past forty-five years." When the choir and officers reached the platform, the president of the Camp Meeting Association "declared the Camp Meeting for the season closed, 'in the name of the Father, and of the Son, and of the Holy Ghost.'"[80]

In the first year the *Ocean Grove Record* was published, a march around the campgrounds was already a feature of the closing service. The president of the association and fifty ministers walked off the preacher's stand arm in arm. The congregation followed them in a procession that circled the auditorium twice. As they marched they sang,

> In the sweet by-and-by,
> We shall meet on that beautiful shore. (*NSC,* 88)

When they returned to the stand, they greeted each other and shook hands before singing the Doxology. Then the bell tolled three times, and the camp meeting was declared over.[81]

According to the 1882 account, those who remained in the auditorium were led by some of the "best singers," who "arranged themselves at the front of the platform and kept up singing for a half hour until the march was concluded." This article also records the origin of a practice—the Ocean Grove salute—still included in the closing ceremonies today.

> At the close of camp meeting, after a hearty hand-shaking, and just before march, a man ran to the platform and said, "Let all here who accept the words uttered by Dr. Stokes this morning, and who now wish to express for him a hearty greeting and 'God bless you,' wave your handkerchiefs."[82]

Until the 1890s, newspaper accounts record that the procession still circled the auditorium two or three times, while singing "We're Marching to Zion," "In the Sweet By-and-By," and "Beulah Land."

In 1912, the march was headed by the Salvation Army band, which was in Ocean Grove to participate in a memorial for Army founder General William Booth.[83] The route and closing activities are consistent with Daniels's account of a few years later, except he does not specifically mention the model. However, the 1914 account in the *Ocean Grove Times* does note the "customary march around the miniature Jerusalem." Although it had become "customary" to include the model in this processional march, this is the first explicit reference in the newspaper to a march around it.[84]

The service marking the end of the camp-meeting revival often took place on Labor Day, which also closed the summer season at Ocean Grove. The Monday holiday meant that guests could stay for a long weekend, even if they were only at Ocean Grove for the days of revival. The last procession around "Jerusalem" occurred on Labor Day in 1959.[85] The following year, camp meeting closed on Sunday evening before Labor Day. In the evening farewell service, the procession was omitted, while some of the features of the morning service were retained, such as the ringing of the bells, the waving of handkerchiefs, and the pronouncement by the president.[86] The singing of the "Hallelujah" chorus, which had become the centerpiece of the Sunday evening service, now took the place of marching and hymn singing around the grounds.[87] The new schedule accommodated the changing reality of summer-vacation schedules and school openings. For many, summer is over long before Labor Day, and today, the week of camp meeting occurs in July or early August. Recently, the community has reinstituted a march on Labor Day to officially mark the close of the season at Ocean Grove, but it no longer culminates camp-meeting week and takes place after many summer guests have already left the Grove.

Closing marches around the campgrounds had been a camp-meeting tradition since the early nineteenth century. On the frontier, this ritual followed a "love feast," where the newly converted were formally welcomed into the Christian body. The march celebrated the unity of these new believers with the rest of the congregation. It also ritually marked the boundaries—temporal and spatial—of the camp-meeting assembly and provided a means for crossing those boundaries. After marching around the perimeter of the meeting grounds, participants heard the official announcement that the meeting was concluded. This marked the end of revival time and facilitated the unification of the camp-meeting fellowship with the larger community. Bruce's excellent description of these marches includes a firsthand account by William Swayze from 1816.

> The meeting closed on Monday morning with exhortation; after which people formed themselves into a large ring two deep, and marched

around the camp ground, within the tents. They took leave of the preachers as they passed. Nothing of this nature could have been more affecting. Some came weeping and others shouting for joy; while some who had no religion wept and cried for bitterness of heart. The oldest preacher pronounced a blessing on the assembly; who then parted from each other in harmony and love.[88]

Daniels's account, written a century after Swayze's, records a remarkable similarity between the marching ceremonies of the two eras, despite very different locations—from frontier to seaside. The assembly continued to take leave of one another with the exchange of greetings, handshaking, and singing, while marching around the site of their "conquest."[89]

The participation of everyone at Ocean Grove in the greeting, singing, and marching of the closing ritual was in contrast to other rituals at frontier camp meetings. Throughout most of these earlier meetings, people were divided physically and functionally into preachers, exhorters, mourners, men, women, black, and white. Bruce interprets the common activity of the closing march as evidence of an understanding of the assembly as the communion of saints, a unity of believers that transcended barriers of time, denomination, and geography. He says, "In fact, there is even evidence that racial barriers were temporarily lifted in the 'singing ecstasy' with which camp-meetings were brought to a close."[90] Johnson concurs that the plank partition that separated the races in antebellum camp meetings "was torn down on the final meeting day when the two peoples joined together in a song festival and 'marching ceremony.' "[91]

For the people of Ocean Grove, Christian unity was an essential element of modeling perfection. Although the community was dominated by white, middle-class Methodists, the presence of people of other denominations, classes, and races was evidence for some of the perfection they sought. When the Godfreys, a Presbyterian family, bought a cottage in 1875, the *Ocean Grove Record* reported, "They were quite at home here, because denominational names and sects were lost sight of in the sweet fellowship of Christian love. This community assembled at the Grove, embracing persons of various creeds. [E]ven Roman Catholics, were pleased to mingle with us, antedat[ing] the coming millennium."[92] In fact, Ocean Grove prided itself on having no "color line." The Association claimed to make no distinction between the "colors" anywhere at Ocean Grove. And blacks were guests in the pulpit as early as 1876.[93] But if the color line was not as visible as the plank partition and separate seating on the frontier, it nevertheless existed at Ocean Grove. Stokes welcomed black preachers and conferences of black churches.[94] However, the trustees encountered opposition from private hotel operators who refused to house black guests.[95] Current residents recall that nearly all black people in Ocean Grove were hotel workers who had to live outside the gates or in the basements of the establishments where they worked. Stokes, however, saw the closing ceremonies of camp-meeting week in 1884 as an opportunity to state explicitly his vision of the coming perfection, when Christians of all races and creeds would gather around one table in the city of God.[96] When several blacks came forward to receive communion, Stokes encouraged them, saying, "Let them come! . . . let the children of Africa, and the dwellers of Asia, and those of Europe and America—let all come, for this is a feast for all nations, and nearly every tribe and tongue has representatives in this vast congregation!"[97] The close of camp meeting, both on the frontier and at Ocean Grove, signaled a time when the congregation could model the communion of saints they anticipated in God's realm but that they often failed to realize even in their assemblies.

The communion of the saints here and now implied the communion of saints across time. A common theme of the closing hymns was the coming reunion of the faithful in heaven.

> Oh, may we meet in heaven;
>> In heaven alone, no sorrow is found,
> And there's no parting there.[98]

In addition to "Marching to Zion," departing Ocean Grove congregations also sang "Onward Christian Soldiers":

> Onward Christian soldiers!
>> Marching as to war,
> With the cross of Jesus
>> Going on before. . . .

> We are not divided,
>> All in body we,
> One in hope and doctrine,
>> One in Charity. (*FW,* 110)

And, "When the Roll Is Called up Yonder":

> On that bright and cloudless morning
>> When the dead in Christ shall rise,
> And the glory of His resurrection share;

> When His chosen ones shall gather
>> To their home beyond the skies,
> And the roll is called up yonder, I'll be there.[99]

The imagery expressed in these hymns told the newly converted that they had become part of an eternal community.[100] For the holiness Methodists at Ocean Grove, the hymnody of the heavenly Jerusalem conveyed a confidence that the members of the perfected community of Jerusalem-by-the-sea were, in fact, the true citizens of Zion and that they would certainly meet once again "in the sweet by and by . . . on that beautiful shore."[101]

The relationship to an eternal community gave the saints a new way of looking at themselves. During camp meeting, they had succeeded in making the new Jerusalem manifest on earth. As a community of the perfected, Ocean Grove had more in common with the eternal heavenly city than with the secular world beyond its gates.[102] Bruce argues that if the closing ceremony objectified the unity of the converted on one level, it also had "strong sectarian overtones."[103] To be chosen to live in harmony with the other saints of New Jerusalem implied that some were not chosen. Being restored spiritually with the rest of the saints meant breaking ties with profane institutions and affirming one's heavenly citizenship.

At the center of this performance of Jerusalem-by-the-sea was the model of Jerusalem. While singing about the new Jerusalem to come, the procession made its way from the auditorium, around Jerusalem-by-the-sea, to Jerusalem (the model), and back to the auditorium. According to Marin, the model was the position of highest importance along the route.[104] The perfected people of God were marching toward the model city prepared for them. A perfectly accurate image of the actual Jerusalem awaited them, conveniently uninhabited, detached from its political matrix, and restored on the New Jersey coast. The circularity of the procession route also suggests the reversibility of this movement: Jerusalem was indeed where they were going, but it was also where they had been. Jerusalem, the model, and Ocean Grove were all the same site on this pilgrimage.

For the Christians of Ocean Grove, the process of perfection required the continual construction of models to identify that perfection for the self. These models, constituted through performance, made explicit what perfection was while simultaneously requiring it. Creating the model also created performers who conformed to the model. But modeling the self was also modeling the Other. In this case, a quite literal model allowed Christians to model a pilgrimage to another city on the other side of the world. That pilgrimage, even though it never left Ocean Grove, transformed the pilgrims, who became, as shown in the drawing in the annual report of 1881 (fig. 24), first-century Jews in nineteenth-century Jerusalem. Performing perfection in this way projected Ocean Grove residents teleologically toward their goal. Modeling oneself in Jerusalem was modeling oneself on the other side of perfection.

EPILOGUE

The opening of the gates of Ocean Grove to Sunday vehicular traffic, in January 1980, symbolized for longtime residents the end of an era. The world outside could no longer be held at bay. Anyone, anytime could enter the gates of holiness. The commingling of sacred and secular times, spaces, and people violated the very core of Ocean Grove's holiness identity. From the outset, its founders had intended the boundaries to hold against all the forces of the world that were inimical to the pursuit of holiness. Whether these forces were the incessant demands of an industrial economy, the crowds of newly arrived immigrants with different beliefs and behaviors, the unhealthy urban environment, the intellectual challenges of science and liberal Christianity, the political freedom of protofeminists, or the sins of male intemperance, they had, with some degree of effectiveness, been performed out of Ocean Grove society. Policemen stood at the gates and bridges, ushers at every auditorium door, and women at the thresholds of the tent city.

Within these boundaries, Ocean Grove had performed itself perfect. Not perfect in the sense that everything always happened the way the trustees of the Ocean Grove Camp Meeting Association would have liked. Rather, perfection in Ocean Grove was distinctly Wesleyan. An individual could claim to stand in right relation to God regardless of the incidental slips that might prove otherwise. Phoebe Palmer's reworking of Wesleyan perfection provided a practical framework for masses of the faithful to reach what once only a saintly few could attempt to attain. Her altar theology suggested

127

that the faithful needed only to claim perfection, and it would be theirs. The Tuesday holiness meeting allowed its participants to reach perfection through its members' own testimonies of perfection.

Ocean Grove was the Methodist parlor society writ large. It was an intentional gathering of like-minded evangelicals who came together to seek holiness through hearing and doing the testimonies of perfection. These testimonies were given daily through constructions in time and space, through bathing and marching, through singing and community pageantry. Even at one square mile, this "parlor" was small enough that mutual accountability was a given; one's every action was displayed and recorded.

The system of performances of holy leisure in Ocean Grove allowed the residents to testify to perfection by modeling it. These models displayed perfection so people could see and understand what it was. They located perfection in the everyday life of Ocean Grovers and enabled them to assume it by performing it. The genius of Ocean Grove was in extending holiness from the parlor prayer meeting to the beach. Conservative evangelicals discovered a moral imperative to enjoy rest and recreation. Conceiving leisure as a means of grace, Grovers performed themselves to perfection and enjoyed themselves while doing so.

So where is holy leisure in Ocean Grove today? Did it die at the turn of the century, when the energy of the holiness movement moved to new denominations? Did Ocean Grove survive the waning of other seaside resorts like Coney Island and the emergence of popular theme parks at midcentury? How can the camp meeting resist secularization, now that the gates are down?

Has a century and a quarter of holy leisure actually produced a different community, or different people?

In short, where do you find perfection?

Even if the 1990s are not the 1890s, the residue of holiness seekers still rests on much of Ocean Grove. The architecture of holiness permeates its streets and public spaces. Staying in the Sampler Inn today requires the same accountability to neighbors that all boarding hotels in Ocean Grove required a century ago. The front row of tent residents can no more escape the preaching of Dr. James Forbes today than they could Billy Sunday's famous sermons ringing through the auditorium doors a century ago. The few "modern" apartments and cottages sit uncomfortably adjacent to restored gems of Victorian resort architecture. The religious meeting halls and pristine white beaches still dominate the landscape and remain the twin poles of Ocean Grove life.

Every summer, the Ocean Grove Camp Meeting Association continues to sponsor Tabernacle Bible Hours, Gospel Concerts, Thornley Chapel's children's programs, Sunday services with well-known Christian speakers, and an annual camp meeting—all according to a schedule hardly changed from the 1870s. And the fruits of the spirit are still evident. People preach, pray, and sing. The auditorium is packed to the rafters during the annual choir festival, and thousands attend every major summer service there. Lou Daniels, music director for the camp meeting, reminds us that many things occur without public knowledge; although they are dealt with quietly, demons are released and people healed. Only fifteen years ago, a "healing meeting" lasted all night.

Today, however, many of the cottages have been insulated to house year-round residents, some of whom pursue businesses quite independent of the Camp Meeting Association's schedule. The modeling agency, hardware store, dentist office, and others follow a calendar determined more by the economics of the Jersey shore than the mythic significance of the ancient Hebrews' wilderness wanderings. Yet all of Ocean Grove bends to the rhythms of the ebb and flow of camp-meeting time. Even the secularized Sundays of Ocean Grove in the 1990s are marked by beach and store closings and the influx of thousands for the preaching services in the auditorium.

If these holiness traditions remain, what of the holiness people? Is Ocean Grove indeed populated by people different from those who are not exposed to these rhythms, this architecture, the beaches, meetings, and community activities? Few of Ocean Grove's current citizens, permanent or temporary, would describe themselves as among the perfected. Yet the people of Ocean Grove, almost without exception, consider this community unique, and many live here or return each summer, generation after generation.

The stories Grovers tell or write about themselves resemble the official annual reports of the Camp Meeting Association. When asked to talk about Ocean Grove, they invariably begin with the creation story: "Ocean Grove was founded in 1869 by people of great vision who hoped to . . . " This consistency is not surprising given the longevity of many Ocean Grove residents. Richard Gibbons, for example, interviewed people from the first generation of the community for the history he published with his wife in 1939. Today, as the unofficial "town historian," Gibbons still writes the weekly column "Retrospect" in the *Ocean Grove Times*. His consistent depiction of Ocean Grove as a place divinely blessed is part of a body of "testimony" that continues to recognize the holy as an enduring feature of this community.

In these stories of Ocean Grove, people frequently cite the sense of community that the place engenders. Indeed, there is a remarkable degree of volunteerism and neighborliness. In a town of less than five thousand year-round residents, a large percentage are actively involved in making the place safer and more hospitable. For example, the all-volunteer company of seventy-five firefighters can respond within minutes to approximately 150 calls a year. Every year at Christmas, Santa rides with the firefighters down Main Avenue to Fireman's Park, where the firefighters hand out apples, oranges, and hard candy; later, they visit shut-ins throughout the community.

Then there is the Ladies Auxiliary to the Auditorium Ushers, an organization of between 150 and 175 wives, widows, and aunts of the ushers that raises $25,000 to $30,000 annually for community causes. Members work all year to arrange the details of the annual bazaar, fish-and-chips dinner, plant sale, and tea. The monies they raise support building renovations, public parks, and youth programs, as well as the activities of the ushers.

Although the duties of the Ocean Grove police force have now been assumed by Neptune Township, Grovers have not diminished their commitment to guard God's square mile. A few years ago, after his son was robbed, an Ocean Grove resident determined that he would patrol the streets himself every night. The volunteer Ocean Grove Citizens' Patrol soon grew to 120 members, who now patrol the streets every night, 365 days a year. This neighborhood-watch program is connected by radio to the Neptune police. Like Ocean Grove's guards a century ago, they patrol the streets looking for people or activities that don't belong in this community.

Like many communities shaped by a strong religious tradition, there is an official and an unofficial Ocean Grove. That is, some in the community cling tenaciously to traditional devotional practice, while others quietly live lives in the same place with little concern for its religious heritage. Dedicated tent residents seem intent on preserving a way of life that has vanished from most other permanent camp meetings, and the ushers still monitor the coming and going of guests to every meeting. In truth, individuals at Ocean Grove have always represented varying degrees of commitment to the ideals of holiness theology espoused by the Camp Meeting Association. From the outset, some came more for the recreation than the religion. Current residents recall the clear distinctions between the "benies"—the summer guests who enjoyed all the benefits of the camp meeting—and the year-round residents who supported these activities with their stores and hotels. Yet the performances of holy leisure permitted and encompassed a range of residents, pilgrims, and vacationers.

Today, the diversity of Ocean Grove's residents and visitors is greater than ever and is evident in striking juxtapositions. Near Victorian cottages occupied by the same family for generations are luxury condominium developments, rooming houses subsidized by state payments to the mentally ill, and a growing enclave of gay residents. Although many voices prophesied the fall of Ocean Grove in 1980, this has not happened. True, the mammoth Model of Jerusalem has long since fallen into disrepair and been dismantled, and few, if any, residents mistake Ocean Grove of the 1990s for the heavenly city. But in some ways, today's Ocean Grove is closer to the nineteenth-century ideal of the millennial community it sought to become. The postbellum holiness seekers imagined a society where faith overcame difference. In Zion, Presbyterians and Baptists could sit at the table with Methodists, blacks and whites could join hands in praising God, and people of every economic class could live side by side in similar dwellings. The nineteenth-century reality in Ocean Grove was a community that withdrew from the cultural, religious, and economic pluralism of the cities to a closed resort with fewer differences. Today, however, many forces at Ocean Grove work against this kind of exclusivity. The newspaper no longer feels obligated to announce that a Presbyterian has bought a cottage. Instead, Methodists share Camp Meeting Week with Presbyterian Day, Baptist Day, Lutheran Day, A. M. E. Day, and Roman Catholic Day. The challenge facing Ocean Grove is to see the diversity reflected in Camp Meeting Week and the new faces moving into Ocean Grove as opportunities rather than threats. The Camp Meeting Association might, for example, engage the gay community in dialogue and ministry.

As the town becomes increasingly a year-round community, with summer guests staying fewer days and returning less often, the rhythms of holy leisure are blurred. New temporal patterns may need to evolve to facilitate holy leisure in the next century. Yet if Ocean Grove is to maintain its identity, it must remember its holy days and holy times. The end of the Sunday-parking ban eroded the weekly pattern of work and quiet, a pattern that the whole community could *feel* in their bodies. Rest was not just a theological idea; it was something their bodies had to do every Sunday. Though a return to the pre-1980 Sunday stillness seems unlikely, a Sunday pedestrian mall on Ocean Pathway or Main Avenue might rekindle the visceral sense of holy times. Certainly the reinstatement of the Labor Day closing march is a step in this direction. Performing beginnings and endings is a key component of self-identity.

As the Grove struggles once again to define itself in light of these and other changes, new performances are emerging that model visions of the community for itself. The restoration of performances from the last century tends to create a model of Ocean Grove lifted out of its current struggles with increasing diversity, liberal Methodism, municipal politics, and the changing economy and ecology of the New Jersey shore. The emphasis on "correct" architectural restoration, the crystallization of the town's history into a foundational myth, and a preference for occasional replays of the "old ways" suggest that Ocean Grove is increasingly modeling its past as a way to shape itself for the future. The need to attract a continual stream of tourists—religious and otherwise—may in fact account for the persistence of some of its Victorian-era characteristics. To what extent, we might ask, is Ocean Grove becoming a historical reconstruction of a holiness camp meeting (à la colonial Williamsburg)? Are the open tent flaps inviting us to gaze on a living exhibit in a museum display of Victorian religious culture? Or do the changes throughout Ocean Grove suggest that the camp-meeting model is continuing to evolve to meet the needs of a third century of holiness seekers? The performance of history—whether through architectural preservation, the historical society, or the Ushers' March—is actually a means of making it so. Modeling the Victorian camp meeting by the sea is the way Ocean Grove continues to shape its future by performing it.

APPENDIX A

CHARTER OF ASSOCIATION

An Act to Incorporate the Ocean Grove Camp Meeting Association of the Methodist Episcopal Church

Section 1: Be it enacted by the Senate and General Assembly of the State of New Jersey, That Ellwood H. Stokes, Ruliff V. Lawrence, George Hughes, William B. Osborn, David H. Brown, John S. Inskip, William H. Boole, Benjamin M. Adams, Alfred Cookman, Adam Wallace, John H. Stockton, Aaron E. Ballard, William Franklin, Robert J. Andrews, Joseph H. Thornl[e]y, George W. Evans, Christopher Sickler, George Granklin, Samuel T. Williams, Willian Manahan, John Martin, George W. Cheeseman, James Black, Oliver L. Gardner, Gardiner Howland, and William F. Jordan and their successors, are hereby constituted a body, corporate and politic, under the name of "The Ocean Grove Camp-Meeting Association of the Methodist Episcopal Church," for the purpose of providing and maintaining, for the members and friends of the Methodist Episcopal Church, a proper, convenient, and desirable permanent Camp-Meeting ground and Christian seaside resort.

Section 2: And be it enacted, That is shall and may be lawful for said corporation to purchase and hold real and personal estate, and to acquire such lands in this State in fee simple or otherwise, as they may deem necessary, proper, or desirable for the purposes and objects of the corporation, and the same or any part thereof to dispose of in parcels or otherwise or in fee simple or otherwise, on such terms, conditions, and restrictions, not repugnant to the laws of this State, or of the United States, as they may see fit.

Section 3: And be it enacted, That it shall be lawful for said corporation to construct and provide all necessary works to supply the said premises with water and artificial light, and to provide all other conveniences and make all other improvements which may be deemed necessary or desirable.

Section 4: And be it enacted, That the affairs of the said corporation shall be managed by twenty-six trustees; the persons named in the first section of this Act shall be the first Trustees of said corporation, and shall hold their offices until others are chosen in their stead—they and their successors shall be and remain members of the Methodist Episcopal Church, in good and regular standing. Any trustee dying, or ceasing to be a member of said church, or being guilty of conduct deemed incompatible with the objects and purposes of the corporation, his place may be declared vacant, and a successor duly elected by a two-thirds vote, by ballot, of the remaining Trustees present at the regular annual meeting of the Association.

Section 5: And be it enacted, That the said Board of Trustees shall from their own number elect a President, Secretary and Treasurer annually, and may appoint any other officers of the corporation they may think proper, from time to time, and may pass and enforce such By-Laws as they may deem needful—provided that the same be not repugnant to the Constitution or laws of this State or of the United States.

Section 6: And be it enacted, That the real and personal property of said corporations (said property not to exceed in annual value five thousand dollars) shall be exempt from all assessment and taxation. Any surplus funds remaining to the corporation, after defraying the expenses thereof, for improvements, or otherwise, shall be devoted to such charitable, benevolent, or religious objects or purposes, as may be agreed on by said Board of Trustees at their regular annual meeting.

Section 7: And be it enacted, That said Trustees shall have the power to appoint such peace officers as shall be deemed necessary for the purpose of keeping order on the Camp-grounds and premises of the corporation, which officers shall be paid by said corporation for their services; but shall have when on duty, the same power, authority, and immunities which constables and other peace officers under the laws of this State possess or enjoy, when on duty as such, and they shall have power to enforce obedience on said grounds and premises to any rule or regulation of said Trustees for the preservation of quiet and good order. All the provisions of "An Act for Supressing Vice and Immorality," revision approved April fifteenth, eighteen hundred and forty-six; and of "An Act to prevent the disturbance of meetings held for the purpose of religious worship," passed February second, eighteen hundred and twenty, shall apply to all meetings or gatherings held in pursuance of, and under the authority of the corporation hereby created, in all respects.

Section 8: And be it enacted, That the meetings of religious services held on said Camp-ground and premises shall, at all times, be under the directions of a committee for that purpose, to be appointed by the said Board of Trustees at their regular annual meeting.

Section 9: And be it enacted, That this act shall be considered a public act, and shall take effect immediately.

Approved: March 3, 1870

BY-LAWS

"The By-Laws declare the objects of the Association to be as follows: 'To provide for the holding of Camp Meetings of an elevated character, especially for the promotion of Christian holiness and to afford to those who would spend a few days or weeks at the seashore an opportunity to do so at moderate cost, free from temptations to dissipation usually found at fashionable watering places.'"[1]

APPENDIX C

RULES AND REGULATIONS OF THE

OCEAN GROVE CAMP MEETING ASSOCIATION

OF THE UNITED METHODIST CHURCH

NOTE: This document has been reproduced in its original form, including occasional errors.

On March 3, 1870, the founding fathers of the Ocean Grove Camp Meeting Association of the United Methodist Church (hereinafter referred to as the "Association") were granted a charter "for the purpose of providing and maintaining for the members and friends of the Methodist Episcopal (now United Methodist) Church, a proper, convenient and desirable permanent Camp Meeting Grounds and Christian seaside resort."

To this end, the following Rules and Regulations are adopted by the Board of Trustees of the Association to which all of the lands of the Camp Grounds commonly known as "Ocean Grove" are described as follows:

Bounded on the East by the Atlantic Ocean; on the North by Wesley Lake and extending westwardly along the major Wesley Lake storm drain right-of-way to a point in the middle of Main Street; on the West by the center line of Main Street; on the South by Fletcher Lake and extending westwardly along the major Fletcher Lake storm drain right-of-way to a point in the middle of Main Street, (which hereinafter is referred to as the "Camp Grounds"), are hereby made subject as appropriate by specific terms of the various leases (including ground leases) with the Association. It should be further understood that these Rules and Regulations are in addition to any and all ordinances of the Township of Neptune or laws or regulations of any other governmental or quasi-governmental body having jurisdiction.

Rules and Regulations Applicable to All Properties Within the Camp Grounds

1. The Sale of, or the Consumption of Alcoholic Beverage On the Premises of a Public Place Is Strictly Prohibited

No person, corporation or other entity within the limits of Camp Grounds, shall sell, barter or dispense for a consideration, any alcoholic beverage, either wholesale or retail, by the bottle, can, glass or in any other manner. This rule shall not apply to medicine having an alcoholic content sold by any licensed drugstore. The prohibition of this rule shall specifically apply to any business or establishment which must hold a license granted by the New Jersey Division of Alcohol Beverage Control Board.

No person, corporation or other entity leasing or operating a restaurant, dining room or other public place where food or liquid refreshments are sold or served to the general public on the Camp Ground shall permit the consumption of alcoholic beverages on such premises.

The term "alcoholic beverages" for the purposes of this rule shall include all forms of liquor, beer, wine and any other spiritous, vinous, malt, brewed or fermented liquor or mixed liquors which contain one-half of one per centum or more of alcohol by volume and which are used or are to be used for beverage purposes.

2. Property Uses Permitted

The following uses of real estate will be permitted on premises located within the Camp Grounds under and subject to all applicable zoning laws of the Township of Neptune.

A. One family dwellings detached
B. Two family dwellings detached
C. Three family dwellings detached
D. Rooming houses
E. Garden apartments
F. Attached row or townhouses
G. Hotels and motels
H. Multi-family apartment houses and condominiums
I. Tent cabins with canvas fronts
J. Retail business establishments of a neighborhood type
K. Retail stores and banks

L. Museums, galleries, and gift shops
M. Personal service establishments
N. Coffee shops, restaurants, and light food concessions
O. Professional and business offices
P. Laundromats and coin-operated dry cleaning establishments
Q. Motion picture theatres
R. Public or private parking facilities
S. Nursing homes and shelter health care facilities
T. Public buildings such as houses for worship, libraries, firehouses and post offices
U. Light impact commercial establishments which sell, repair, or service automobiles and wholesale distribution establishments provided said establishments front on Main Street
V. Parks, playgrounds and similar public or semi-public recreation facilities provided such facilities are deemed by the Board of Trustees to be compatible with the objects of the Association.

The Association may grant additional uses by vote of the Board of Trustees or of its Executive Committee. Any such uses shall be considered on a case-by-case basis and shall be limited in effect to the premises for which such additional use is granted. Any additional use granted in one case shall not be construed as an indication that the same exception or use shall be granted in another case. The grant of any additional use may be made subject to such conditions or restrictions as the Association believes are reasonable and in the best interest of the Association or the community.

3. Change from Existing Use

Whenever any leaseholder or sub-lessee shall desire to change the use of a leased property, whether or not said use is specifically permitted by Article 2 hereof, said person shall first obtain the written consent of the Association. Such consent shall not be considered an endorsement of the use at the particular location for zoning purposes. The Association may address an objection or an endorsement of the use to the Zoning Board of the Township of Neptune when the Association wishes to take a position as to the appropriateness of the use at the particular location, even though the proposed use is one permitted on the Camp Grounds under Section 2 hereof.

4. Construction on Sunday Prohibited

Except in cases of emergency consisting of a condition threatening a clear and present danger to persons or property and only then with the written permission of the Association, no leaseholder or sub-lessee of any lot shall construct, erect, repair, make alteration to, do external painting, demolish or remove, (or cause or permit any other person, guest or invitee to do such work) of or to any building, or structure of any kind, whether attached to or severed from the land, upon any premises located on the Camp Grounds, on the first day of the week commonly known as Sunday.

5. (Reserved for Future Use)

6. Buildings

Any construction, alteration, addition or repair to any building, outbuilding or other lot improvement within the Camp Grounds and for which work a building or other type permit is required by the Township of Neptune, shall first be approved by the Association. With the approval of any such work, the Association may attach such conditions or restrictions as it believes are reasonable and in the best interests of the Association or the community.

7. (Reserved for Future Use)

8. Parking of Motor Vehicles, Trailers or the Storage of Boats

No motor vehicle, trailer or boat shall be parked or stored on any setback or open space lying between a leased lot and the curb or curb line of the street, avenue, lane, ways or places upon which such leased lot shall front. Corner lots shall be considered as fronting on both intersecting streets, avenues, lanes, ways or places and through lots shall be considered to front at both ends. The holder of a leased lot to which this section applies not only shall refrain from parking on such area, but shall also not permit others to park thereon. This prohibition shall not apply to ground within the leased lot boundaries.

9. Maintenance of Sidewalks, Curbs, Street Trees, Yards and Plantings

A. It shall be the duty of all lessees of lots fronting on any of the streets, avenues, lanes, ways, or places within the premises of said Association to construct sidewalks in front of the same of either concrete or flagging of the width and at the grade established by the Township of Neptune (if any) and to properly curb the same, and to keep the sidewalks which are now constructed, or may hereafter be constructed, and the curbs along the same in front of these lots in proper repair and safe for travel. If the sidewalks and curbs along said lots shall not be constructed or repaired as aforesaid, or shall not be of the proper grade or width, the said Association shall have authority through its Executive Director to notify said lessees to construct, repair or relay the same with either flagging or concrete, and if said lessee or

lessees shall refuse or neglect to construct, repair or relay the same as aforesaid within twenty days after being so notified, the said Association may
construct, repair or relay the same and collect the expense thereof from the
lessee or lessees by action at law, or may add the same to the annual assessment on said lot made against lessee or lessees, with legal interest thereon.
The failure of the Association to take action hereunder shall not relieve
the lessee of the obligation hereby imposed. Corner lots shall be considered
fronting on both intersecting streets, avenues, lanes, ways or places and
through lots shall be considered to front at both ends.

B. It shall be the duty of all lessees of lots fronting on any of the streets,
avenues, lanes, ways or places within the premises of said Association to
maintain any trees, yards and plantings in front of the same in a manner
which shall meet the codes and ordinances of the Township of Neptune and
protect the welfare and safety of the public, and to afford neighboring lots
an unrestricted view of the ocean within the first two blocks therefrom, and
if the trees, yards and plantings shall not be maintained as aforesaid, the
Association shall have authority through its Executive Director to notify
lessees to properly maintain the same, and if the lessee or lessees shall refuse
or neglect to maintain the same aforesaid within twenty days after being
so notified, the Association may perform such maintenance and collect the
expense thereof from the lessee or lessees by action at law or may add the
same to the annual assessment on said lot made against the lessee or lessees,
with legal interest thereon. The failure of the Association to take action
hereunder shall not relieve the lessee of the obligation hereby imposed.

C. It shall be the duty of all lessees of lots fronting on any of the streets,
avenues, lanes, ways or places within the premises of said Association
to maintain sidewalks in front of the same by keeping them free of debris,
obstruction, snow, or ice or any other substance which may present a
danger to pedestrian traffic.

10. (Reserved for Future Use)

Rules and Regulations Applicable to Parks, Grassed Promenades, and Other Areas Intended for Public Use Which Are Under the Jurisdiction of the Association

11. Alcohol and Drugs Prohibited
The consumption of alcoholic beverages of any kind or description, use of
marijuana or any other natural or chemical substances which tend to alter
the rational mind processes (commonly known as "drugs") is prohibited.

12. *Littering Prohibited*

Littering is prohibited. For purposes of this Rule and Regulation the term "Littering" shall include (but not be limited to) the deposit of solid excrement by any pet. The owner of the pet, whether or not present shall be responsible and shall make provision for the removal of such excrement.

13. *Riding of Bicycles Prohibited*

Riding of skateboards, pedal bicycles, motorized bicycles or other motorized vehicles, except equipment for handicapped persons, on pedestrian walkways (excepting the boardwalk as outlined in Rule 23) or on grassed areas is prohibited.

14. *Sleeping at Night Prohibited*

Sleeping on grassed areas, sidewalks or park benches during the night hours of 10:00 P.M. to 7:00 A.M. is prohibited.

15. *Camping Prohibited*

Any form of camping is prohibited in these areas. For this purpose the term "camping" shall not include picnicking provided no open fire is used.

16 through 20. *(Reserved for Future Use)*

Rules and Regulations Applicable to the Boardwalk and Beach

21. *Alcohol and Drugs Prohibited*

The consumption of alcoholic beverages of any kind or description, the use of marijuana or any other natural or chemical substances which tend to alter the rational mind processes (commonly known as "drugs") is prohibited.

22. *Dogs Prohibited During the Summer*

Dogs shall not be permitted on the beaches or boardwalk at any time of the day from the first day of June through the fifteenth day of September.

23. *Pedal Bicycles*

Riding of pedal bicycles on the boardwalk is prohibited at all times except between the hours of 3:00 A.M. to 10:00 A.M.

24. *Motorized Vehicles Prohibited*

Automobiles, motorcycles, motorbikes and any other type of motorized vehicle (except equipment for handicapped persons) are prohibited from riding or parking on the boardwalk or beach. Maintenance or work type vehicles while engaged in such maintenance or work will be permitted with the written consent of the Association subject to such restrictions as the Association may wish to impose for the prevention of damage to property or safety of persons.

25. Sleeping at Night Prohibited
Sleeping on the beach, boardwalk or benches on the boardwalk during the hours 10:00 P.M. to 7:00 A.M. is prohibited.

26. Swimming on Unguarded Beaches Prohibited
Swimming, rafting or surfing from an unguarded beach is prohibited. Persons swimming, rafting or surfing from an unguarded beach shall be trespassers; and the Association shall have no responsibility for their safety.

27. Use of the Beach and Guarded Beaches
The Association will establish hours for the use of the beach and the hours for swimming on guarded beaches. Persons using the beaches shall be subject to regulations and restrictions in guarded areas as may be imposed by the lifeguard on duty at any time and from time to time depending upon his or her judgment of surf conditions, and swimmer safety.

28. Beach Fees
Fees for the use of the beaches during established hours will be fixed by the Association annually.

29. Surfing
Surfing on surf boards or other rigid flotation devices may be conducted only if and for so long as the Association designates a "surfing beach"; and then, and only then, on such designated beach and at such times when it is guarded. Persons surfing from any other beach, or at times when a "surfing beach," if any, is not guarded, shall be trespassers and the Association shall have no responsibility for their safety.

30. Bathing Tags
Bathing tags or other proof of payment of the beach entrance fee shall be worn by all bathers on the beach during established hours in the summer season.

31. Entrance to the Beach
Entrance to the beach shall only be gained through entranceways provided in the railing on the boardwalk.

32. No One Permitted on Beaches Sunday Morning During Summer

No one will be permitted on the beaches from 9:00 A.M. to 12:30 P.M. on Sundays commencing with the second Sunday of June to and including the second Sunday of September.

33. Beach Parties

Persons desiring to have a beach party at any time other than the hours established for swimming during the summer season, shall first obtain written permission from the Association which shall fix a fee for such permission. Any written permission for a beach party shall be strictly under and subject to the rules hereof. In addition the Association, through its representative issuing the permit, may impose such additional restrictions on said permission as may be necessary to protect and preserve the interests of the Association or the community.

34. Open Fires on the Beach

Open fires on the beach at any time are prohibited except upon written permission of the Association. A permit for a beach party issued under the preceding paragraph 33 shall specify whether it includes permission for an open fire. Any open fire on the beach with Association permission shall be under and subject to regulation by the local Board of Fire Commissioners.

35. Commerce on the Beach and Boardwalk

No person may offer for sale, or sell any article, commodity, beverage, food or perform any service for which such person anticipates payment, either on the beach or the boardwalk except with the written permission of the Association. All such activity is also under and subject to zoning and mercantile license regulations of the Township of Neptune.

36. Use of Beach and Boardwalk a Privilege

The use of the beach and boardwalk by the public is considered by the Association as the extension of a privilege to the user. The Association reserves the right through its authorized representative/s to withdraw that privilege from any person (whether or not such person paid an entrance fee) who misuses that privilege by violating any of the above rules, or for indecent exposure, inappropriate display, abusive act or language directed to another user or a representative of the Association, destruction of property, conduct considered hazardous to other persons or property, or for any other conduct which is not generally considered compatible with the interest or purposes of the Association or interests of the community.

The standard for the application of the terms "indecent exposure," "inappropriate display" and "abusive act or language" as used in the preceding sentence shall be the generally accepted standard for the community of Ocean Grove in keeping with the stated purpose of the Association being to provide and maintain "for members and friends of the Methodist Episcopal (now United Methodist) Church, a proper, convenient and desirable permanent Camp Meeting Grounds and Christian seaside resort."

37 through 50. (Reserved for Future Use)

Miscellaneous

51. Headings for Convenience Only
The descriptive headings in these Rules and Regulations are inserted for convenience only and shall not control or affect the meaning or construction of any of the provisions hereof.

52. Unenforceable Provisions
If any section or provision of these Rules and Regulations or the application thereof to any person or circumstances shall to any extent be held to be invalid, illegal or unenforceable, the remaining provisions or the application of such term or provision to persons or circumstances other than those as to which it is held invalid, illegal or unenforceable, shall not be affected thereby, and each remaining term and provision hereof shall be valid and enforced to the fullest extent permitted by law.

53. Amendment
The Association reserves to itself the right to amend, repeal, or adopt additions to these Rules and Regulations at any time and from time to time, but such amendment, repeal or adoption shall only be by specific action of the Board of Trustees of the Association.

54. Enforcement
The Association will use reasonable efforts to enforce the provisions of these Rules and Regulations within its limited resources. Enforcement may take the form of forfeiture of the lease hold interest as provided in the lease, or such other civil or criminal remedies as may be available to the Association. Failure to enforce or delay in enforcement will not be construed as a waiver of the right of the Association to subsequently enforce these Rules and Regulations. Neither the Association nor any of its Trustees, Officers, or

employees will be liable to any person, corporation or entity for the failure to enforce these Rules and Regulations.

55. Repealer and Adoption

With certain deletions, these Rules and Regulations constitute a codification and republication of existing Rules and Regulations which were adopted by the Association at the time the decision of the Supreme Court of New Jersey became effective in the case of State vs. Celmer and which has formerly been Ordinances of the Association. To this end, all Rules and Regulations heretofore adopted by the Association are hereby repealed and replaced by the adoption of these Rules and Regulations hereinabove recited.

Adopted this 31st day of December, 1992.
Philip C. Herr II, President
Walter A. Ouigg, Secretary

1. Setting the Stage

1. Kenneth Brown, *Holy Ground: A Study of the American Camp Meeting*, 25.

2. Charles Johnson, *The Frontier Camp Meeting*, 25.

3. Ibid., 242.

4. Ibid., 249.

5. Brown, *Holy Ground* and "Finding America's Oldest Camp Meeting," *Methodist History* 25, no. 4 (July 1990), 252–54.

6. "Sacramental" services included the observance of Holy Communion.

7. Russell E. Richey, "From Quarterly to Camp Meeting: A Reconsideration of Early American Methodism," *Methodist History* 23, no. 1 (July 1985), 199–213.

8. Ibid., 200.

9. John Wesley, *Letters*, VIII, 238, as quoted in Colin Williams, *John Wesley's Theology Today*, 167.

10. Dickson Bruce Jr., *And They All Sang Hallelujah: Plain-Folk Camp-Meeting Religion, 1800–1845*, 69–70.

11. Melvin Easterday Dieter, *The Holiness Revival of the Nineteenth Century*, 24.

12. *Journal of the General Conference of the Methodist Episcopal Church, 1832*, as quoted in Dieter, *Holiness Revival*, 25.

13. D. Gregory Van Dussen, "The Bergen Camp Meeting in the American Holiness Movement," *Methodist History* 21, no. 2 (January 1983), 69ff.

14. At a national holiness conference in 1877, Rev. C. W. Ketchem, for example, feels compelled to defend the practice of calling "special" meetings for

the promotion of holiness. "On the one hand it is said, 'all our religious services are for the promotion of holiness,' and it would sound strange to call a meeting for 'the promotion of justification by faith, or the witness of the Spirit, or any one of the special doctrines of our holy religion.' And yet the only objection to this kind of a call may be our unfamiliarity with it. . . . There is directness of object, unity of aim and feeling, heartiness of devotion, and strength of desire, as well as freedom from the restraints of a promiscuous assembly, which are evidently greatly in favor of these special meetings." "Methods to Be Used, and the Proprieties to Be Regarded in Spreading Scriptural Holiness Throughout the Land," *Proceedings of Holiness Conferences*, 109.

15. Dieter, *Holiness Revival*, 2.

16. Ibid., 18–19, 28–32.

17. David Kinnear, *Christian Holiness*, 15.

18. Dieter, *Holiness Revival*, 98–99.

19. On the origins of holiness camp meetings, see Dieter, *Holiness Revival*, 104ff.; Percival Wesche, "The Revival of the Camp-Meeting by the Holiness Groups," Chap. 7; and E. Dale Dunlap, "Tuesday Meetings, Camp Meetings, and Cabinet Meetings: A Perspective on the Holiness Movement in the Methodist Church in the United States in the Nineteenth Century," *Methodist History* 13, no. 3 (April 1975), 94–95.

20. Charles A. Parker, "The Camp Meeting on the Frontier and the Methodist Religious Resort in the East—Before 1900," *Methodist History* 18, no. 3 (April 1980), 184.

21. Dieter, *Holiness Revival*, 101.

22. Morris Daniels, *The Story of Ocean Grove*, 23–24, and Mr. and Mrs. Richard F. Gibbons, *History of Ocean Grove, 1869–1939*, 10–11.

23. Daniels, *Story*, 25.

24. Ibid.

25. Ibid., 24.

26. Gibbons, *History*, 9.

27. Daniels, *Story*, 40.

28. Ibid., 42.

29. Richard Brewer, *Perspectives on Ocean Grove*, 15.

30. As quoted in Brewer, *Perspectives*, 17.

31. Daniels, *Story*, 134.

32. Bruce, *Hallelujah*, 71.

33. The use of "men" here and elsewhere is intentional. Although women were at the forefront of the holiness movement and active at Ocean Grove as preachers, exhorters, and teachers, the Ocean Grove Camp Meeting Association was, at first, limited to male trustees. Women at Ocean Grove enthusiastically supported the temperance and suffrage movements and bore considerable responsibility for shaping the community even in its infancy. (It was Mrs. Thornley, after all, who called the first religious service.) There were, however, significant

differences in the roles available to men and women. See chapter 5 for a further discussion of this issue.

34. Gibbons, *History*, 45.

35. Daniels, *Story*, 179.

36. Ibid., 181.

37. Ibid., 182.

38. Stephen Crane, "On the New-Jersey Coast: Summer Dwellers at Asbury Park and Their Doings," *New York Tribune*, 24 July 1892, 22.

39. *Asbury Park Press*, July 21, 1992, C1.

40. Glenn Uminowicz, "Recreation in Christian America," in *Hard at Play*, ed. Kathryn Grover, 30.

41. Ibid., 8ff. 25.

42. Gibbons, *History*, 62.

43. Catherine Bell, *Ritual Theory, Ritual Practice*, 184–86.

44. Dona Brown, *Inventing New England: Regional Tourism in the Nineteenth Century*, 6, 75–104.

45. Ibid., 6.

46. Uminowicz, "Recreation," 8, 34.

47. Tom McGrath, "Discover the Jersey Shore," *US Air Magazine*, 1, no. 7 (summer 1994), 38–39.

48. Don Handelman, *Models and Mirrors: Towards an Anthropology of Public Events*.

2. Holy Rhythms

1. "Professional entertainment did not begin to bring the excitement of the outside world to town and rural residents on a steady basis until the early twentieth century." Ted Ownby, *Subduing Satan: Religion, Recreation, & Manhood in the Rural South*, 39.

2. B. W. Gorham, *Camp Meeting Manual*, 124.

3. Brooks McNamara, "Popular Scenography," *The Drama Review* 18, no. 1, (March 1974), 24.

4. Johnson, *Frontier*, 208ff.

5. Nineteenth-century diaries and letters reveal that patterns of family attendance at rural camp meetings varied greatly—from the optimal week away with the family to occasional visits to the revival site. For example, in his diary entries of 30 July–3 August 1869, Caleb Edward Iddings records sporadic attendance, with and without his family, over five days. Thomas Owen, on the other hand, wrote to John Owen on 1 October 1820 about the reactions of all his family members to the camp meeting they had attended for several days.

6. Johnson, *Frontier*, 209.

7. Mary R. Campbell, letter to William B. Campbell, 10 October 1826.

8. William George Matton, memoirs, Chap. 5. Around 1868, Matton describes a camp meeting that was invaded by "rowdies," two men from respected

families in the community; the local constable was reluctant to act. The meeting organizers had taken precautions to avoid such disruptions, but the whiskey sellers got in anyway. The account describes how Matton, a preacher at the meeting, helped grab the two men, get an injunction against them, and send them on their way.

9. Roger Robins, "Vernacular American Landscape: Methodists, Camp Meetings, and Social Responsibility," *Religion and American Culture* 4, no. 2 (summer 1994), 165.

10. Randall Balmer, "From Frontier Phenomenon to Victorian Institution: The Methodist Camp Meeting in Ocean Grove, New Jersey," *Methodist History* 25, no. 3 (April 1987), 200.

11. Robins, "Vernacular Landscape," 167.

12. Johnson presents a widely held assumption that the emergence of these manuals was evidence of the disintegration of camp meetings (Johnson *Frontier,* 249). Kenneth Brown and other more recent scholars dispute that assessment, arguing that the camp meetings were vital forms in and of themselves even if they had considerably modified the original concept. Brown also includes a comprehensive bibliography and list of currently active camp meetings to underscore the vitality of this form of revivalism (Brown, *Holy Ground*).

13. Gorham, *Manual,* 155–56.

14. Parker, "Religious Resort," 172.

15. Ibid., 176.

16. Rev. H. Vincent, *History of the Camp-Meeting Grounds at Wesleyan Grove, Martha's Vineyard, for the eleven years ending with the Meeting of 1869,* 44.

17. Robins, *Vernacular Landscape,* 178.

18. *Vineyard Gazette,* 31 August 1866, as quoted in Kenneth Brown, *Holy Ground,* 93.

19. Kenneth Brown, *Holy Ground,* 95.

20. *Ocean Grove Record,* 25 August 1875, 2.

21. Parker, "Religious Resort," 190.

22. *Ocean Grove Record,* 7 July 1883, 2.

23. Ibid., 12 August 1876, 339.

24. Mircea Eliade, *The Sacred and the Profane: The Nature of Religion,* 85.

25. Lev. 23:43, Deut. 16:14–15, Neh. 8:14–17.

26. Gorham, *Manual,* 30–31.

27. Vincent, *Wesleyan Grove,* 80.

28. Matt. 4:1, Mark 1:12, Luke 4:1.

29. "And after he had dismissed the crowds, he went up the mountain by himself to pray" (Matt. 14:23). "In the morning, while it was still very dark, he got up and went out to a deserted place, and there he prayed" (Mark 1:35). "Now during those days he went out to the mountain to pray; and he spent the night in prayer to God" (Luke 6:12). "Six days later, Jesus took with him Peter and James and John, and led them up a high mountain apart, by themselves" (Mark 9:2a).

30. Gorham, *Manual*, 38.

31. *Ocean Grove Record*, 25 June 1875, 2.

32. Thomas Owen, letter to John Owen, 8 November 1800.

33. *Ocean Grove Record*, 18 June 1875, 2.

34. Bruce, *Hallelujah*, 126.

35. Kenneth Brown, "Leadership in the National Holiness Association with Special Reference to Eschatology, 1867–1919" (Ph.D. diss., Drew University, 1988), 286.

36. Ibid., 284.

37. "He Being Dead Yet Speaketh," *Advocate of Christian Holiness*, December 1871, 222–23, as quoted in Kenneth Brown, *Leadership*, 288–89.

38. Eviatar Zerubavel, *Hidden Rhythms: Schedules and Calendars in Social Life*, 109.

39. Ibid., 119ff.

40. Ownby, *Subduing Satan*, 106ff. Evangelicals referred to Sunday observances throughout this period as the "Sabbath," even though early Christians were careful to distinguish between the Jewish Sabbath and the Christian "Lord's Day." Equating Sunday with Sabbath allowed Christians to apply the mythic importance of the Jewish Sabbath to their own day of worship.

41. Ibid.

42. Albert Outler, ed., *John Wesley*, 178–79.

43. Daniels, *Story*, 34.

44. *Ocean Grove Times*, 20 May 1876, 242.

3. Holy Space

1. Quotations from early hymnbooks are cited in the text using the following abbreviations: FW—*The Finest of Wheat, No. 2: Hymns New and Old for Missionary and Revival Meetings and Sabbath Schools*, 1894; NSC—*New Starry Crown*, 1872; OGCS—*Ocean Grove Christian Songs*, 1902; OGS—*Ocean Grove Songs*, 1900; VOP—*The Voice of Praise: A Collection of Hymns for Use by the Methodist Church*, 1872.

2. Robins, "Vernacular Landscape," 168.

3. John Jackson, *The Necessity for Ruins*, 81.

4. Ibid., 84.

5. Ibid., 77–88.

6. Gorham, *Manual*, 137. The preference for canvas did not extend to the preacher's tent. This structure, usually under or attached to the pulpit, was invariably constructed of wood. Gorham's manual, like others, gave precise measurements for the necessary lumber. William Matton gives an interesting account of a time when a log "tent" constructed for his family was mistaken for the preacher's tent. His ability to build a replacement out of shingles and clapboard siding in less than four hours gives some indication of both the crudeness of these designs as well as the ease with which they could be constructed. Matton, *Memoirs*, n.p.

7. Ellen Weiss, *City in the Woods: The Life and Design of an American Camp Meeting on Martha's Vineyard,* 25.

8. Ibid., 28.

9. Ibid., 52.

10. *Ocean Grove Record,* 12 August 1976, 339.

11. Uminowicz, "Recreation," 12.

12. Brenda Parnes, "Ocean Grove: A Planned Leisure Environment," in *Planned and Utopian Experiments: Four New Jersey Towns,* ed. Paul A. Stellhorn, 30.

13. Weiss, *City in the Woods,* 71–72.

14. *Ocean Grove Record,* 24 July 1875, 1.

15. Weiss, *City in the Woods,* 69.

16. Inscription on the door of the Abbey Church of St. Denis, the first Gothic structure. Abbot Suger, *On the Abbey Church of St. Denis and Its Art Treasures,* ed. and trans. Erwin Panofsky, 47–49.

17. John Calvin, *Institutes of the Christian Religion,* I.11, 109.

18. *Ocean Grove Record,* 22 May 1880, 1.

19. *History of Ocean Grove: Diamond Jubilee 1869–1944,* 64.

20. *Ocean Grove Record,* 22 July 1876, 301.

21. Dieter, *Holiness Revival,* 45.

22. Daniels, *Story,* 59.

23. Ibid., 58.

24. *Ocean Grove Record,* 22 July 1876, 301.

25. Weiss, *City in the Woods,* 120.

26. Ibid.

27. Because there was some distrust of sectarian utopian communities by the American public in general, the large flag on the auditorium organ was installed after World War I to help alleviate such fears.

28. *Ocean Grove Record,* 1 July 1876, 293.

29. Susan Davis, *Parades and Power: Street Theatre in Nineteenth-Century Philadelphia,* 159.

4. Body and Soul

1. Johnson, *Frontier,* 57.

2. Bruce, *Hallelujah,* 53.

3. Peter Cartwright, *Autobiography of Peter Cartwright, the Backwoods Preacher,* 30.

4. Bruce, *Hallelujah,* 53, 76–77.

5. John Norman Sims, "The Hymnody of the Camp Meeting Tradition" (D.S.M. diss., Union Theological Seminary, New York, 1960), 139–42.

6. In the early nineteenth century, employers provided beer or whiskey for their employees, and merchants had a bottle ready to close any transaction. Roy Rosenzweig, *Eight Hours for What We Will.*

7. Harvey Green, *Fit for America: Health, Fitness, Sport and American Society,* 181.

8. Ibid., 182.

9. Roberta J. Park, "Healthy, Moral, and Strong," in *Fitness in American Culture,* ed. Kathryn Grover, 123ff.

10. Ibid., 139.

11. Ibid., 141.

12. The 1860s saw the establishment of numerous urban athletic clubs, most notably San Francisco's Olympic Club (1866) and the New York Athletic Club (1868). Green, *Fit for America,* 182.

13. Ibid., 183.

14. Ibid.

15. Park, "Healthy, Moral, and Strong," 133.

16. Catharine Beecher, *Physiology and Calisthenics for Schools and Families,* 87.

17. Green, *Fit for America,* 78–80, 84.

18. Ibid., 128.

19. Ibid.

20. See Rosenzweig, *Eight Hours,* 127ff., for a discussion of the park system in Worcester, Mass., as it developed along class lines.

21. Stephen F. Weinstein, "The Nickel Empire: Coney Island and the Creation of Urban Seaside Resorts in the United States" (Ph.D. diss., Columbia University, 1984), 71.

22. Weinstein, "Nickel Empire," 51.

23. Green, *Fit for America,* 54ff.

24. Ibid., 55.

25. Edward Hitchcock, "Warm Bathing," in *Journal of Health* (I: 5, November 11, 1829), as quoted in Green, *Fit for America,* 57.

26. Beecher, *Physiology,* 100.

27. Ibid., 138.

28. D. Brown, *Inventing New England,* 47–48.

29. Alain Corbin, *The Lure of the Sea: The Discovery of the Seaside in the Western World, 1750–1840,* 95.

30. Corbin, *Sea,* 96.

31. D. Brown, *Inventing New England,* 94ff.

32. *Ocean Grove Record,* 15 July 1876, 306.

33. Ibid., 22 July 1882, 2.

34. Corbin, *Sea,* 87.

35. Ibid. See his chapter "A New Harmony between the Body and the Sea."

36. Daniels, *Story,* 149–50.

37. *Ocean Grove Record,* 3 May 1879, 1.

38. Ibid., 22 July 1876, 306.

39. Daniels, *Story,* 259–60.

40. Ibid., 260–61.

41. Gibbons, *History*, 61.
42. Ibid.
43. See, for example, *Voice of Praise*, 865.
44. From an account quoted in John Shaw, *The Great Auditorium Organ*, 8.
45. "Therefore we have been buried with him by baptism into death, so that, just as Christ was raised from the dead by the glory of the Father, so we too might walk in newness of life" (Romans 6:4).
46. Daniels, *Story*, 159.
47. Weiss, *City in the Woods*, 118–21.
48. Ibid., 120.
49. *Ocean Grove Record*, 15 August 1885, 2.
50. *Ocean Grove Times*, 8 August 1903, 1.
51. Gibbons, *History*, 87.
52. Weiss, *City in the Woods*, 119–20.
53. E. H. Stokes as quoted in Brewer, *Perspectives*, 20.
54. Daniels, *Story*, 81–86.
55. Ibid., 82.

5. Male and Female

1. Johnson, *Frontier*, 12.
2. In the early nineteenth century, women were not yet accepted as ministers in the evangelical traditions that fostered camp meetings. By the later nineteenth century, due in large part to holiness leaders like Palmer, preachers were both male and female, as explained later in this chapter.
3. Johnson, *Frontier*, 12–13.
4. Bruce, *Hallelujah*, 33.
5. Ownby, *Subduing Satan*, 22.
6. Ibid., 14–15.
7. Ibid., 4, 7.
8. Ibid., 4.
9. Bruce, *Hallelujah*, 68–69.
10. Ibid., 64.
11. As quoted in Ownby, *Subduing Satan*, 14.
12. Bruce, *Hallelujah*, 132.
13. Barbara Leslie Epstein, *The Politics of Domesticity*, 22.
14. Ibid., 74.
15. Ibid., 76.
16. Ibid., 60–61.
17. Dieter, *Holiness Revival*, 42.
18. At frontier camp meetings, the space immediately in front of the preacher's stand was often reserved for those struggling through the conversion process. Individuals on the verge of conversion would congregate there, either on a bench or in a pen, to receive the prayers and assistance of others. Here,

where the work of conversion became especially intense, women assumed the most direct role in facilitating this rite of passage.

19. *Ocean Grove Times,* 8 June 1912, 1.

20. Mark Wigley, "Untitled: The Housing of Gender," in *Sexuality & Space,* ed. Beatriz Colomina, 332.

21. Weiss, *City in the Woods,* 28.

22. Daniels, *Story,* 236.

23. Green, *Fit for America,* 236.

24. Ibid., 215, 237.

25. Gibbons, *History,* 57. "A greater occasion than 'Roosevelt Day' has never been seen in Ocean Grove in all its history" (Daniels, *Story,* 219).

26. Uminowicz, "Recreation," 25.

27. Daniels, *Story,* 236.

28. Ibid., 63.

29. Ibid., 64.

30. Ibid., 63–64.

31. An usher recalls only a single instance when the organist didn't play the Ushers' March: the head usher refused to give his signal, and the ushers held their ground until the organist relented and played.

32. *Diamond Jubilee History,* 11.

33. *Ocean Grove Times,* 24 August 1934, 1.

34. Ibid., 15 August 1969, 1.

35. Ibid., 25 August 1967, 1.

36. The Seals and Crofts concert of 1974 was a trial run for the Association. The dramatic shift in entertainment prompted numerous letters of opposition in the local paper. See *Ocean Grove Times,* 18 April 1974, 2.

37. Uminowicz, "Recreation," 28.

38. *Ocean Grove Times,* 25 July 1903, 4; 1 August 1903, 1.

39. Ibid., 3 September 1904, 1.

40. Uminowicz, "Recreation," 29.

41. *Ocean Grove Times,* 17 August 1912, 1.

42. Ibid., 24 August 1912, 4.

43. Christine Stansell, "Women, Children, and the Uses of the Streets: Class and Gender Conflicts in New York City, 1850–1860," *Feminist Studies* 8, no. 2 (Summer 1982), 309–36.

44. Ibid., 310.

45. Ibid., 312.

46. Uminowicz, "Recreation," 29.

47. Stansell, "Women, Children, and the Streets," 310.

48. Epstein, *Politics of Domesticity,* 89, 102–4.

49. Ibid., 107.

50. Estelle Freedman, "Separatism As Strategy: Female Institution Building and American Feminism, 1870–1930," *Feminist Studies* 5, no. 3 (fall 1979), 513.

51. Epstein, *Politics of Domesticity*, 115.
52. *Ocean Grove Times*, 25 July 1903, 1.
53. Freedman, "Separatism As Strategy," 515.
54. Ibid.
55. Epstein, *Politics of Domesticity*, 129.
56. Stansell, "Women, Children, and the Streets," 330.

6. Jerusalem by the Sea

1. Gibbons, *History*, 41.
2. *Ocean Grove Record*, 12 July 1879, 2.
3. Lester Vogel, *To See a Promised Land: Americans and the Holy Land in the Nineteenth Century*, 2.
4. Ibid.
5. Ibid.
6. Vogel, *Promised Land*, 3.
7. Ibid.
8. *Ocean Grove Record*, 9 August 1879, 1, 3.
9. Jonas Barish, *The Anti-Theatrical Prejudice*, 295ff.
10. Barbara Kirshenblatt-Gimblett, "Objects of Ethnography," in *The Poetics and Politics of Museum Display*, ed. Ivan Karp and Steven D. Lavine, 397–98.
11. Neil Harris, *Humbug: The Art of P. T. Barnum*, 36.
12. Richey, *Early American Methodism*, 82ff. The author traces the history of "four languages" speaking simultaneously in the voices of early American Methodism. The tensions between these different voices—popular/evangelical, Wesleyan, Episcopal/Anglican, and republican—help Richey account for the diversity within the denomination and the discordance that would develop in the nineteenth century among representatives of the different languages. According to this scheme, the voice of camp meetings is almost exclusively popular/evangelical, although the mature resort camp meetings show a tendency toward republicanism as well.
13. Ibid. See 92ff. for a discussion of this painted text in the architecture of holiness.
14. *Ocean Grove Record*, 22 July 1876, 301.
15. Naomi Shepherd, *The Zealous Intruders*, 80.
16. Ibid., 73, and Vogel, *Promised Land*, 27.
17. Nathan Schur, *Twenty Centuries of Christian Pilgrimage*, 137–47.
18. Shepherd, *Zealous Intruders*, 170–75.
19. Ibid., 177–80.
20. Ibid., 78–79. See also Vogel, *Promised Land*, 3.
21. Shepherd, *Zealous Intruders*, 76.
22. Vogel, *Promised Land*, 233–36.
23. Ibid., 214.
24. Ibid., 215.

25. *Ocean Grove Christian Songs,* 21.

26. *Ocean Grove Record,* May 24, 1879, 1.

27. Ibid., 21 August 1880, 3.

28. Ibid., 30 July 1881, 2.

29. *Annual Report* (1881), 22.

30. Ibid.

31. Gibbons, *History,* 41.

32. Allen Moore, *The Modern City of Jerusalem: As shown by Wythe's Great Model of the Holy City,* title page.

33. John Davis, "Picturing Palestine: The Holy Land in Nineteenth-Century American Art and Culture" (Ph.D. diss., Columbia University, 1991), 11.

34. Ibid.

35. Horatio B. Hackett, *Illustrations of Scripture: Suggested by a Tour through the Holy Land* (Boston: William Heath, 1857), as quoted in Robert T. Handy, ed., *The Holy Land in American Protestant Life, 1800–1948,* 37.

36. William C. Prime, *Tent Life in the Holy Land* (New York: Harper & Brothers, 1857; reprinted by Arno Press, 1977), as quoted in Handy, *The Holy Land,* 108.

37. Gibbons, *History,* 42.

38. *Ocean Grove Times,* 13 July 1912, 1.

39. Kirshenblatt-Gimblett, "Objects of Ethnography," 404.

40. Moore, *Jerusalem.*

41. These sermons may have been preached at Ocean Grove. Brewer records that Talmage, the Presbyterian pastor of the five-thousand-member Brooklyn Tabernacle, was one of the more notable ministers to speak at Ocean Grove in its early years. Brewer, *Perspectives,* 29.

42. T. DeWitt Talmage, *Talmage on Palestine,* 50–51.

43. J. Davis, "Picturing Palestine," 1.

44. Shepherd, *Zealous Intruders,* 99.

45. Ibid., 101, 105.

46. Ibid.

47. Ibid., 105, 191.

48. J. Davis, "Picturing Palestine," 113.

49. *Annual Report* (1891), 28.

50. John Davis, "Holy Land, Holy People? Photography, Semitic Wannabes, and Chautauqua's Palestine Park," *Prospects* 17 (1992), 261.

51. Ibid.

52. J. Davis, "Holy Land, Holy People," 260.

53. Barbara Kirshenblatt-Gimblett, "Objects of Memory: Material Culture As Life Review," in *Folk Groups and Folklore Genres: A Reader,* ed. Elliott Oring, 335.

54. Ibid.

55. Louis Marin, "Notes on a Semiotic Approach to Parade, Cortege, and Procession," in *Time Out of Time,* ed. Alessandro Falassi, 226.

56. Gibbons, *History*, 41.
57. J. Davis, "Picturing Palestine," 106.
58. George D. Elderkin, *The Finest of the Wheat: Hymns Old and New*, 199.
59. *Ocean Grove Record*, 25 August 1883, 2.
60. Bruce, *Hallelujah*, 82–83.
61. *Ocean Grove Record*, 1 September 1883, 1.
62. Ibid., 8 September 1883, 2.
63. Shepherd, *Zealous Intruders*, 78.
64. Kirshenblatt-Gimblett, *Objects of Ethnography*, 397ff.
65. Ibid., 405, 407.
66. Ibid., 89–95.
67. Shepherd, *Zealous Intruders*, 93.
68. Ibid., 93, 98–99.
69. Ibid., 93.
70. *Ocean Grove Record*, 16 August 1884, 2.
71. J. Davis, "Holy Land, Holy People," 242.
72. Ibid., 242–43.
73. Ibid., 264.
74. J. Davis, "Picturing Palestine," 133.
75. Ibid., 264–65.
76. *Ocean Grove Times*, 13 July 1912, 1.
77. J. Davis, "Holy Land, Holy People," 265.
78. Gibbons, *History*, 42.
79. J. Davis, "Holy Land, Holy People," 265.
80. Daniels, *Story*, 53–55.
81. *Ocean Grove Record*, 11 September 1875, 1–2.
82. Ibid., 3 September 1882, 1. Waving handkerchiefs was a silent, "orderly" way to show appreciation. Clapping was considered inappropriate by the late nineteenth century for "respectable" Methodist worship.
83. Ibid., 7 September 1912, 1.
84. Ibid., 1 September 1914, 1.
85. Ibid., 11 September 1959, 1.
86. Ibid., 2 September 1882, 1.
87. *Ocean Grove Times*, 9 September 1960, 2.
88. As quoted in Bruce, *Hallelujah*, 83ff.
89. Daniels, *Story*, 54.
90. Bruce, *Hallelujah*, 89.
91. Johnson, *Frontier*, 46.
92. *Ocean Grove Record*, 18 June 1875, 2.
93. Ibid., 9 July 1887, 2.
94. Ibid., 22 September 1883, 2.
95. Ibid., 24 July 1886, 2. A "Missionary Jubilee" of the African Methodist Episcopal church, attended by "an immense following of intelligent members of

the churches for over 100 miles around, were welcomed to Ocean Grove" by Stokes.

96. Ibid., 22 September 1883, 2. "It is true that some of the proprietors of hotels here objected to receiving these colored men through fear of offending their white guests, but the Association is not to be held responsible for the prejudice of those who visit the Grove, nor for the sacrifice of principles to gain on the part of the hotel proprietors who refused to entertain these gentlemen because of their color."

97. Rev. 8:3, 19:9.

98. *Ocean Grove Record,* 6 September 1884, 2.

99. Bruce, *Hallelujah,* 115.

100. *Ocean Grove Times,* 24 August 1912, 8, and *Ocean Grove Christian Songs,* 70, 89.

101. Bruce, *Hallelujah,* 116.

102. "There's a Land That Is Fairer Than Day," *Voice of Praise,* 956.

103. Bruce, *Hallelujah,* 115. On the frontier, people moved from a status completely outside the church through conversion to membership within the church. The march of the newly converted clearly marked them as members of the church throughout all ages as opposed to the sinners outside the perimeter of tents (Bruce, *Hallelujah,* 116–17). Holiness seekers were similarly separating themselves from a society they viewed as corrupt and claiming membership in a Christian community without temporal bounds.

104. Marin, "Parade," 227.

Appendix B

1. Gibbons, *History,* 81.

BIBLIOGRAPHY

Absolutely Portable Buildings. Grand Rapids, Mich.: Grand Rapids Portable House
    Company, 1887.
Adams, Doug. *Meeting House to Camp Meeting: Toward a History of American Free
    Church Worship from 1620 to 1835.* Saratoga, N.Y., and Austin, Tex.: Modern
    Liturgy-Resource Publications and The Sharing Company, 1981.
Annual Reports of the President of the Ocean Grove Camp-Meeting Association. Ocean
    Grove, N.J.: Ocean Grove Camp Meeting Association, 1874–89.
Balmer, Randall H. "From Frontier Phenomenon to Victorian Institution: The
    Methodist Camp Meeting in Ocean Grove, New Jersey." *Methodist History* 25, no. 3
    (April 1987): 194–200.
Bell, Catherine. *Ritual Theory, Ritual Practice.* New York and Oxford: Oxford University
    Press, 1992.
Bishop, Anne, and Doris Simpson. *The Victorian Seaside Cookbook.* Newark: New Jersey
    Historical Society, 1983.
Bloch, Maurice. *Ritual, History and Power: Selected Papers in Anthropology.* Atlantic
    Highlands, N.J.: The Athlone Press, 1989.
Braithwaite, David. *Fairground Architecture: The World of Amusement Parks, Carnivals,
    and Fairs.* New York: Frederick A. Praeger, 1968.
Brewer, Richard E. *Perspectives on Ocean Grove: Social and Cultural Notes.* Ocean Grove,
    N.J.: Richard E. Brewer, 1987.
Brown, Dona L. *Inventing New England: Regional Tourism in the Nineteenth Century.*
    Washington and London: Smithsonian Institution Press, 1995.
Brown, Kenneth O. "Finding America's Oldest Camp Meeting." *Methodist History* 28,
    no. 4 (July 1990): 252–54.

―――. *Holy Ground: A Study of the American Camp Meeting.* New York: Garland Publishing, 1992.

―――. "Leadership in the National Holiness Association with Special Reference to Eschatology, 1867–1919." Ph.D. diss., Drew University, 1988.

Bruce, Dickson, Jr. *And They All Sang Hallelujah.* Knoxville: University of Tennessee Press, 1974.

Campbell Family Letters, 1822–26. Duke University Divinity School Library Special Collections, Durham, N.C.

Cartwright, Peter. *The Autobiography of Peter Cartwright, the Backwoods Preacher.* New York: Carlton and Porter, 1857.

Corbin, Alain. *The Lure of the Sea: The Discovery of the Seaside in the Western World, 1750–1840.* Cambridge, England: Polity Press, 1994.

Cunningham, John T. "To These Shores." *Ocean Grove Centennial.* Ocean Grove, N.J.: Ocean Grove Camp Meeting Association, 1969.

Daniels, Morris. *The Story of Ocean Grove: Related in the Year of Its Golden Jubilee.* New York and Cincinnati: The Methodist Book Concern, 1919.

Davis, John. "Holy Land, Holy People? Photography, Semitic Wannabes, and Chautauqua's Palestine Park." *Prospects* 17 (1992): 241–72.

―――. "Picturing Palestine: The Holy Land in Nineteenth-Century American Art and Culture." Ph.D. diss., Columbia University, 1991.

Davis, Susan. *Parades and Power: Street Theatre in Nineteenth-Century Philadelphia.* Philadelphia: Temple University Press, 1986.

de Kruiff, Leif Michael. *Twenty Years and Ten Days: "My Life With Grace."* Neptune, N.J.: American Press, 1987.

Dieter, Melvin Easterday. *The Holiness Revival of the Nineteenth Century.* Metuchen, N.J.: Scarecrow Press, 1980.

Dunlap, E. Dale. "Tuesday Meetings, Camp Meetings, and Cabinet Meetings: A Perspective on the Holiness Movement in the Methodist Church in the United States in the Nineteenth Century." *Methodist History* 13, no. 3 (April 1975): 85–106.

Eliade, Mircea. *The Sacred and the Profane: The Nature of Religion.* New York and London: Harcourt, Brace & World, 1959.

Epstein, Barbara Leslie. *The Politics of Domesticity.* Middletown, Conn.: Wesleyan University Press, 1981.

Fankhauser, Craig Charles. "The Heritage of Faith: An Historical Evaluation of the Holiness Movement in America." Ph.D. diss., Pittsburg State University, 1983.

Fraternal Camp-Meeting Sermons Preached by Ministers of the Various Branches of Methodism at the Round Lake Camp-Meeting, New York, July 1874. New York: Nelson & Phillips, 1875.

Freedman, Estelle. "Separatism As Strategy: Female Institution Building and American Feminism, 1870–1930." *Feminist Studies* 5, no. 3 (September 1979): 512–29.

Gibbons, Mr., and Mrs. Richard F. Gibbons. *History of Ocean Grove, 1869–1939.* Ocean Grove, N.J.: Ocean Grove Times, 1939.

Gibbons, Richard F. "Retrospect Recalls Auditorium Ushers' Shows." *Ocean Grove and Neptune Times* (22 August 1991), 7.

Gilbert, Martin. *Jerusalem: Rebirth of a City.* New York: Viking Penguin, Inc., 1985.

Glassberg, David. *American Historical Pageantry: The Uses of Tradition in the Early Twentieth Century.* Chapel Hill: University of North Carolina Press, 1990.

Gorham, Barlow Weed. *Camp Meeting Manual: A Practical Book for the Camp Ground in Two Parts.* Boston: H. V. Degen, 1854.

Green, Harvey. *Fit for America: Health, Fitness, Sport, and American Society.* New York: Pantheon Books, 1986.

Grimes, Ronald. *Beginnings in Ritual Studies.* Lanham, Md.: University Press of America, 1982.

———. *Ritual Criticism: Case Studies in Its Practice, Essays on Its Theory.* Columbia: University of South Carolina Press, 1990.

Grover, Kathryn. *Hard at Play: Leisure in America, 1840–1940.* Amherst, Mass., and Rochester, N.Y.: University of Massachusetts Press and Strong Museum, 1992.

———, ed. *Fitness in American Culture: Images of Health, Sport, and the Body, 1830–1940.* Rochester, N.Y.: Strong Museum, 1989.

Handelman, Don. *Models and Mirrors: Towards an Anthropology of Public Events.* Cambridge: Cambridge University Press, 1990.

Handy, Robert T. *A Christian America: Protestant Hopes and Historical Realities.* New York and Oxford: Oxford University Press, 1984.

———, ed. *The Holy Land in American Protestant Life, 1800–1948.* New York: Arno Press, 1981.

Harris, Neil. *Humbug: The Art of P. T. Barnum.* Boston and Toronto: Little, Brown and Company, 1973.

———, ed. *The Land of Contrasts, 1880–1901.* New York: George Braziller, 1970.

History of Ocean Grove: Diamond Jubilee 1869–1944. Ocean Grove, N.J.: Ocean Grove Times and the Ocean Grove Camp Meeting Association, 1944.

Huizinga, Johan. *Homo Ludens: A Study of the Play Element in Culture.* Boston: Beacon Press, 1950.

Hunton, Gail, and Jennifer Boyd. *A Home Renovator's Guide for Historic Ocean Grove.* Ocean Grove, N.J.: Ocean Grove Home Owner's Association, 1989.

Iddings, Caleb Edward. Diary, 1869. Duke University Divinity School Library Special Collections, Durham, N.C.

Jackson, John B. *Discovering the Vernacular Landscape.* New Haven, Conn., and London: Yale University Press, 1984.

———. *The Necessity for Ruins.* Amherst: University of Massachusetts Press, 1980.

Johnson, Charles A. *The Frontier Camp Meeting.* Dallas: Southern Methodist University Press, 1955.

Jones, Stephen G. *Workers at Play: A Social and Economic History of Leisure, 1918–1939.* London: Routledge & Kegan Paul, 1986.

Kasson, John. *Amusing the Million: Coney Island at the Turn of the Century.* New York: Hill & Wang, 1978.

Kinnear, Rev. David. *Christian Holiness.* Nashville: E. Stevenson & F. A. Owen, 1857.

Kirshenblatt-Gimblett, Barbara. "From Cult to Culture: Jews on Display at World's Fairs." *Plenary Papers: Proceedings of 4th Congress of SIEF (Société Internationale d'Ethnologie et de Folklore).* Bergen, 1990.

———. "Objects of Ethnography." *The Poetics and Politics of Museum Display,* ed. Ivan Karp and Steven D. Lavine. Washington: Smithsonian Institution Press, 1991.

———. "Objects of Memory: Material Culture as Life Review." *Folk Groups and Folklore Genres: A Reader,* ed. Elliott Oring. Logan: Utah State University Press, 1989.

———. "Problems in the Early History of Jewish Folkloristics." *Tenth World Congress of Jewish Studies* 2 (1990): 21–31.

La Penna, Harold. *Hymn Search: A Compendium of Published Articles Concerning Composers and Authors and Their Religious Services at Ocean Grove, New Jersey.* Ocean Grove, N.J.: Harold La Penna, 1994.

Last of the Great Camp Meetings. Producers Jennifer Boyd and John Sosenko. Ocean Grove, N.J.: Community Heritage Film Group, forthcoming documentary film.

Levine, Lawrence W. *Highbrow/Lowbrow: The Emergence of Cultural Hierarchy in America.* Cambridge, Mass.: Harvard University Press, 1988.

Lindley, Kenneth. *Seaside Architecture.* London: Hugh Evelyn, 1973.

Marin, Louis. "Notes on a Semiotic Approach to Parade, Cortege, and Procession." *Time Out of Time,* ed. Alessandro Falassi. Albuquerque: University of New Mexico Press, 1987.

Massebeau, W. A. *The Camp Meeting in South Carolina Methodism.* Greenwood, S.C.: Order of the Societies, 1919.

Matton, William George. *Memoirs, 1883.* Duke University Divinity School Library Special Collections, Durham, N.C.

McMahon, T. J. *The Golden Age of the Monmouth County Shore.* Fair Haven, N.J.: T. J. McMahon, 1964.

McNamara, Brooks. "Popular Scenography." *The Drama Review* 18, no. 1 (T-61) (March 1974), 16–24.

Moore, Allen. *The Modern City of Jerusalem: As Shown by Wythe's Great Model of the Holy City.* Ocean Grove, N.J.: n.p., c. 1930.

Moore, Sally F., and Barbara G. Myerhoff. *Secular Ritual.* Assen, The Netherlands: Van Gorcum, 1977.

Osborn, Lucy Reed Drake. *Pioneer Days of Ocean Grove.* New York: The Methodist Book Concern, 1915.

Outler, Albert, ed. *John Wesley.* Oxford: Oxford University Press, 1964.

Owen, Thomas. *Letters, 1800–1820.* Duke University Divinity School Library Special Collections, Durham, N.C.

Ownby, Ted. *Subduing Satan: Religion, Recreation, and Manhood in the Rural South.* Chapel Hill: University of North Carolina Press, 1990.

Parker, Charles A. "The Camp Meeting on the Frontier and the Methodist Religious Resort in the East—Before 1900." *Methodist History* 18, no. 3 (April 1980): 179–92.

Peiss, Kathy. *Cheap Amusements: Working Women and Leisure in Turn-of-the-Century New York*. Philadelphia: Temple University Press, 1986.

Peters, John L. *Christian Perfection and American Methodism*. New York: Abingdon Press, 1956.

Proceedings of Holiness Conferences. Philadelphia: National Publishing Association for the Promotion of Holiness, 1877.

Richey, Russell E. *Early American Methodism*. Bloomington and Indianapolis: Indiana University Press, 1991.

———. "From Quarterly to Camp Meeting: A Reconsideration of Early American Methodism." *Methodist History* 23, no. 1 (July 1985): 199–213.

Robins, Roger. "Vernacular American Landscape: Methodists, Camp Meetings, and Social Responsibility." *Religion and American Culture* 4, no. 2 (June 1994): 165–91.

Rosenzweig, Roy. *Eight Hours for What We Will*. Cambridge: Cambridge University Press, 1983.

Rosser, Rev. L. *Class Meetings: Embracing Their Origin, Nature, Obligation, and Benefits*. Richmond, Va.: Rev. L. Rosser, 1855.

Schechner, Richard. *The Future of Ritual: Writings on Culture and Performance*. New York: Routledge, 1993.

Schur, Nathan. *Twenty Centuries of Christian Pilgrimage*. Tel Aviv: Dvir Publishing House, 1992.

Shaw, John R. *The Great Auditorium Organ*. Ocean Grove, N.J.: Ocean Grove Camp Meeting Association, 1995.

Shepherd, Naomi. *The Zealous Intruders*. San Francisco: Harper & Row, 1987.

Smith, Jeanne Jacoby. *An Altar in the Forest: A History of Mount Lebanon Campmeeting, 1892–1992*. Lebanon, Penn.: Mt. Lebanon Campmeeting Association, 1990.

Smith, Timothy. *Revivalism and Social Reform: American Protestantism on the Eve of the Civil War*. Baltimore and London: Johns Hopkins University Press, 1957.

Stansell, Christine. "Women, Children, and the Uses of the Streets: Class and Gender Conflicts in New York City, 1850–1860." *Feminist Studies* 8, no. 2 (June 1982): 309–36.

Stellhorn, Paul A. , ed. *Planned and Utopian Experiments: Four New Jersey Towns*. Trenton: New Jersey Historical Commission, 1980.

Stokes, Ellwood Haines. *Footprints in My Own Life*. Asbury Park, N.J.: M. W. & C. Pennypacker, 1898.

Talmage, T. De Witt. *Talmage on Palestine*. Springfield, Ohio: Mast, Crowell & Kirkpatrick, 1890.

Thompson, George. *A View of the Holy Land, Its Present Inhabitants, Their Manners and Customs, Polity and Religion*. Wheeling, Va.: John B. Wolff, 1850.

Turner, Victor. *From Ritual to Theatre: The Human Seriousness of Play*. New York: Performing Arts Journal Publications, 1982.

———. *The Ritual Process*. Hawthorne, N.Y.: Aldine Publishing Company, 1969.

Van Dussen, D. Gregory. "The Bergen Camp Meeting in the American Holiness Movement." *Methodist History* 21, no. 2 (January 1983), 69–89.

Vincent, Hebron. *History of the Camp-Meeting Grounds at Wesleyan Grove, Martha's Vineyard, for the Eleven Years Ending with the Meeting of 1869.* Boston: Lee and Shepard, 1870.

———. *History of the Wesleyan Grove Camp Meeting from the First Meeting Held There in 1835 to That of 1858.* Boston: George C. Rand and Avery, 1858.

Vogel, Lester I. *To See a Promised Land: Americans and the Holy Land in the Nineteenth Century.* University Park: Pennsylvania State University Press, 1993.

Weinstein, Stephen F. "The Nickel Empire: Coney Island and the Creation of Urban Seaside Resorts in the United States." Ph.D. diss., Columbia University, 1984.

Weiss, Ellen. *City in the Woods: The Life and Design of an American Camp Meeting on Martha's Vineyard.* New York and Oxford: Oxford University Press, 1987.

Wesche, Percival A. "The Revival of the Camp-Meeting by the Holiness Groups." Ph.D. diss., University of Chicago, 1945.

Whorton, James. *Crusaders for Fitness: The History of American Health Reformers.* Princeton, N.J.: Princeton University Press, 1982.

Wigley, Mark. "Untitled: The Housing of Gender." *Sexuality and Space,* ed. Beatriz Colomina. Princeton, N.J.: Princeton University School of Architecture, 1990.

Williams, Susan. *Savory Suppers and Fashionable Feasts: Dining in Victorian America.* New York: Pantheon Books, 1985.

Zerubavel, Eviatar. *Hidden Rhythms: Schedules and Calendars in Social Life.* Berkeley: University of California Press, 1981.

INDEX

altar theology, 10, 127

annual reports, of the Ocean Grove Camp
    Meeting Association, 18, 106, 110,
    111, 125, 129

Asbury Park, New Jersey, x, 19–21, 23,
    25, 59, 94, 95; carousel, x, 21; ferris
    wheel, 19

Atlantic City, New Jersey, 4

auditorium, 13, 17, 23, 35, 36, 45, 53,
    55, 92, 93, 100, 116, 120, 121, 125,
    127, 129; first, 45; Great Auditorium,
    20, 41, 63, 99, 120; third, 17. *See also*
    Ladies Auxiliary to the Auditorium
    Ushers; Ushers

Baby Parade, 26, 36, 94–96

Balmer, Randall, 33

band, in Ocean Grove, xii

Barnum, P. T., 102

Beecher, Catharine, 66, 67, 69, 71

Beecher, Henry Ward, 34, 104

Beecher, Lyman, 66

Bell, Catherine, 24

boats, procession of illuminated, 36. *See
    also* Lake Carnival

Booth, Catherine, 87

Booth, William, 122

Bradley, James, 20, 95

Bradley Beach, New Jersey, 19, 20, 23, 120

Brighton Beach, New York, 68, 120

Brown, Dona, 25, 70, 71

Brown, Kenneth, 5, 6, 39

Brown, Tom, 67

Bruce, Dickson, Jr., 9, 24, 39, 64, 84–86,
    122, 123, 125

Burford, Robert, 104, 105

Calvin, John, 51

Cane Ridge, Kentucky, 5, 6, 21, 37, 63, 64

Cape May, New Jersey, 13

Carnival Queen, 95

Carnival Week, 36, 95

Cartwright, Peter, 64

Cash, W. J., 85

Celmer, Louis, Jr., 23

Centennial Park, in Ocean Grove, 121

167

TROY MESSENGER is the Director of Worship and a lecturer at Union Theological Seminary. Messenger received his Ph.D. in performance studies from New York University and holds an M.Div. and M.A.R. from Yale Divinity School. Ordained as a Baptist minister, he has served on the staff of several churches in the Northeast.